SUMMARY OF POWER PRAYERS

40 Devotions and Declarations to Reverse Impossible Situations

JUDY JACOBS

D DESTINY IMAGE

Destiny Image P.O. Box 310, Shippensburg, PA 17257-0310

This book and all other Destiny Image's books are available at Christian bookstores and distributors worldwide.

For Worldwide Distribution.

Reach us on the Internet: www.destinyimage.com.

ISBN 13 TP: 9798881501488

ISBN 13 eBook: 9798881501495

CONTENTS

INTRODUCTION

In the spiritual journey of every believer, prayer stands as the pivotal force that brings heaven's power into earthly challenges. "Power Prayers" is not just a book; it's a spiritual toolkit designed to equip believers with the understanding and insight needed to unlock profound dialogues with the Divine. This book delves into the essence of effective prayer, revealing how it transforms not only circumstances but the very hearts of those who engage in it.

Through the pages of "Power Prayers," readers are introduced to the multifaceted dimensions of prayer. It teaches that prayer is more than a ritual; it is the active practice of connecting with God on a personal level, presenting our desires, fears, hopes, and gratitude, thus embodying the lifeline of a thriving faith. The book outlines structured prayers for various needs and situations, emphasizing that prayer is both an armor in times of war and a balm in moments of peace.

The essence of "Power Prayers" lies in its ability to guide readers through the complexities of different types of prayers—intercession, supplication, thanksgiving, and praise—while anchoring each type in biblical truths. It showcases powerful testimonies and biblical narratives that exemplify the impact of prayer, encouraging readers to step into a deeper, more strategic prayer life.

This introduction aims to prepare you for a transformative journey. As you flip through the summaries of each chapter, expect to find key insights that will challenge and enhance your understanding of prayer. You'll discover practical tips that can be applied immediately, deep spiritual truths to meditate on, and dynamic prayer strategies that promise to elevate your spiritual walk.

"Power Prayers" serves as a reminder that our prayers, whether whispered in the quiet corners of our homes or declared boldly in community gatherings, hold the power to move mountains. By the end of this book, you'll not only learn about the power inherent in prayer but also how to wield it effectively to see real change in your life and the lives of those around you. Prepare to be transformed by the renewing power of strategic and heartfelt prayer.

CHAPTER 1

BEYOND DESPERATION— FAITH

Bible Verse

"For I know the thoughts that I think toward you, says the Lord, thoughts of peace and not of evil, to give you a future and a hope." —Jeremiah 29:11 (NKJV)

Introduction

This chapter explores how moments of desperation can reveal our true selves and push us to pursue God with greater intensity. Whether facing personal, family, or health struggles, desperation often drives us to seek answers from God with an unwavering commitment to faith. The author invites readers to embrace the transformative power of faith during life's challenging seasons, urging them to hold onto their "until" moments—staying firm in prayer, belief, and trust until their breakthrough arrives.

Word of Wisdom

"Faith causes you to become strong in every area of your life. The more truth and steadfastness you have, the more true and steadfast you will be." Judy Jacobs

Main Theme

The chapter emphasizes that faith, rooted in prayer, is the key to overcoming desperate situations. By staying persistent in faith—praying, believing, and standing "until" the answer comes—believers can witness life-changing miracles and experience God's promises in full.

Key Points

- Desperation brings out the real you, especially in hard and unexpected circumstances.
- People often turn to drastic measures when desperate, from diets to saving marriages.
- Desperation can sometimes lead to enabling behaviors, especially in family relationships.
- The secret to overcoming challenges is persistence—praying, believing, and standing firm until the answer comes.
- Faith is the foundation for stability and strength in every area of life.

- Victory comes through faith, rooted in the promises of God and the truth of His Word.

Key Themes

- Desperation often uncovers who we truly are and pushes us to act in ways we normally wouldn't. It can drive people to take extreme measures in health, relationships, and personal situations, revealing our deep longing for change.
- Breakthroughs in life require a steadfast commitment to keep praying, believing, and standing in faith until the answer arrives. The author encourages readers to hold onto their faith and focus on the promise of an eventual breakthrough, no matter how long it takes.
- The author reflects on how faith, rooted in the Bible, is solid and true. It is not a fairy tale but something to be grounded in, providing stability and strength in every aspect of life, especially during difficult times.
- While some things remain hidden in God's wisdom, there are many promises revealed to us in Scripture that we can claim. The author reminds readers that these promises are for them and their descendants, encouraging a legacy of faith.
- The chapter emphasizes that prayer is the key to accessing all that God has in store for us. A desperate heart, when aligned with persistent prayer and unwavering faith, will see God's hand move in powerful

ways, resulting in victory and answered prayers.

Conclusion

This chapter calls readers to embrace the power of faith during desperate times, urging them to stand firm in prayer until they see the victory they desire. The author encourages believers to stay focused on God's promises and reminds them that break-through is on the other side of their 'until.' Desperation can be a catalyst for deeper faith and reliance on God's unfailing provision.

CHAPTER 2

THE COST

Bible Verse

"For which of you, intending to build a tower, does not sit down first and count the cost, whether he has enough to finish it—lest, after he has laid the foundation, and is not able to finish, all who see it begin to mock him, saying, 'This man began to build and was not able to finish'?" —Luke 14:28-30 (NKJV)

Introduction

This chapter delves into the profound sacrifices required to follow Jesus Christ, drawing parallels between everyday decisions about resources and the spiritual commitment of discipleship. The author shares personal stories to illustrate the deep emotional and practical investments involved in following Christ, marriage, parenting, and overcoming personal tragedies.

Word of Wisdom

"It will cost you everything to follow Jesus, but He is worth every sacrifice."
Judy Jacobs

Main Theme

The central theme explores the notion that true discipleship and life's most profound commitments require complete surrender and often come at a high cost, but ultimately lead to immeasurable spiritual rewards.

Key Points

- Understanding the cost is crucial before beginning any significant endeavor, whether building a house, engaging in warfare, or following Christ.
- Committing to something significant, like discipleship or marriage, requires a thorough understanding of the required sacrifices.
- Loss and pain are sometimes part of the journey, yet they contribute to our spiritual growth and resilience.
- The greatest investments in life, especially spiritual ones, demand everything we have, including our time, resources, and heart.
- The rewards of such commitments are eternal, making the sacrifices worthwhile.

- The personal cost of discipleship can manifest in many forms, including emotional and practical challenges.

Key Themes

- **Counting the Cost in Discipleship:** Just as one calculates the cost before building a house or going to war, the author emphasizes the need to assess what following Jesus will entail. This calculation is not about discouraging commitment but ensuring readiness and willingness to give up everything for the sake of Christ.
- **Personal Sacrifices for Greater Good:** The author shares personal anecdotes, such as the emotional journey of marriage and the pain of a miscarriage, to highlight that life's most meaningful commitments often come with significant challenges and sacrifices, yet they lead to deeper fulfillment and spiritual growth.
- **Surrender and Loss as Pathways to Faith:** Experiencing loss, such as the miscarriage the author describes, tests one's faith but also strengthens reliance on God's sovereignty. These trials are portrayed not just as tests, but as opportunities to deepen one's faith and understanding of God's ultimate plan.
- **The Price Tag of Life's Choices:** Every major decision carries a price tag, from adopting a pet to deciding to follow Christ. The author uses the metaphor of a hidden

price tag to discuss the often unseen costs associated with our choices, emphasizing the need for careful consideration and spiritual wisdom.

- **Eternal Rewards of Earthly Sacrifices:** The narrative reassures that while the costs of discipleship and personal sacrifices are high, the spiritual and eternal rewards far outweigh these earthly challenges. This perspective encourages readers to endure hardships with faith and hope for divine compensation.

Conclusion

The chapter concludes with a powerful affirmation of the worthiness of following Jesus, despite the high costs it may entail. The author encourages readers to embrace the challenges and sacrifices of discipleship, assuring them that the rewards, both in this life and beyond, are greater than any temporary hardships. Through personal reflection and biblical wisdom, readers are invited to count the cost and commit deeply to their faith, knowing that their sacrifices pave the way for eternal joy and fulfillment.

CHAPTER 3

TIMING

Bible Verse

"My times are in your hands; deliver me from the
hands of my enemies, from those who pursue me."
—Psalm 31:15 (NIV)

Introduction

This chapter reflects on the crucial role of
divine timing in life's events, highlighting
how moments are orchestrated for our
growth and to fulfill God's plan. Through personal
anecdotes about family and challenges, the author
conveys the importance of trusting God's timing,
especially during periods of waiting and uncertainty.

Word of Wisdom

"The timing of the Lord was every-
thing for me in waiting on my until mo-
ment, and your until moment will always

involve waiting on the Lord's timing and faithing it!" Judy Jacobs

Main Theme

The main theme revolves around the belief that God's timing is perfect, even when it seems delayed or unclear from our perspective. Life's significant events, whether joyous or challenging, occur exactly when they should to fulfill God's purpose in our lives.

Key Points

- Life's pivotal moments, such as the birth of a child or overcoming fear, are dictated by divine timing.
- Personal experiences and challenges teach the importance of patience and trust in God's perfect schedule.
- God's view of our life's timeline is complete, seeing from beginning to end, unlike our limited perspective.
- Prayer is a powerful tool that aligns us with God's timing and plans for us.
- Trust in God's timing can transform fear and anxiety into peace and purpose.
- Waiting on God requires faith and active engagement through prayer.

Key Themes

- **Divine Timing in Personal Milestones:** The births of the author's children and the challenges they faced underscore that significant life events happen not only at the right time but also serve greater purposes. These moments of joy and trial are used to illustrate how every event is a part of God's meticulous plan.

- **Prayer as Connection and Conduit:** Prayer is emphasized as an essential practice that not only connects us deeply with God but also acts as a conduit through which His plans are revealed and realized. The author shares how prayer elevated her ability to cope with her daughter's fears, transforming anxiety into triumph.

- **Perception versus Reality in Divine Timing:** While humans often see timing as linear and immediate, God views our lives comprehensively, knowing the best moments for each event to unfold. This perspective encourages readers to trust in God's oversight and perfect knowledge of our lives.

- **Challenges as Opportunities for Growth:** The difficulties faced by the author's daughter and their resolution through faith and prayer are portrayed as opportunities for spiritual and personal growth. These experiences highlight the transformative power of trusting in God's timing.

- **Faith in God's Plan Amid Uncertainty:** The narrative encourages embracing uncertainty with faith, trusting that God's timing often means waiting patiently for the right moment. This trust is crucial for overcoming doubts and fears when outcomes are not immediately visible.

Conclusion

In conclusion, the chapter reinforces the message that trusting in God's perfect timing is essential for navigating life's challenges and receiving His best for us. By accepting that our timelines are securely in God's hands, we can live with peace and confidence, knowing that every moment of our lives is purposefully orchestrated for our ultimate good and His glory.

CHAPTER 4

A WRESTLING

Bible Verse

"I can do all things through Christ who strengthens me." —Philippians 4:13 (AMPC)

Introduction

This chapter explores the intense struggle between faith and the flesh, describing the author's personal experiences of wrestling with doubts and fears while standing firm in faith. It highlights the mental and spiritual battles faced when clinging to God's promises despite the enemy's lies, using personal anecdotes to demonstrate the power of persistent faith.

Word of Wisdom

"I have strength for all things in Christ Who empowers me; I am ready for anything and equal to anything through

Him Who infuses inner strength into me."
Judy Jacobs

Main Theme

The chapter delves into the concept that faith often requires a struggle against one's own doubts and fears, emphasizing that through Christ's strength, believers can endure and overcome these challenges.

Key Points

- The flesh and faith are constantly at odds, presenting a persistent battle for believers.
- The enemy often uses lies to undermine faith, but these can be overcome through the power of Christ.
- Persistent intercession is a costly but ultimately rewarding aspect of faith.
- Personal conviction and confession are crucial in overcoming spiritual battles.
- The support of family and community is essential but must be complemented by personal faith.
- Victory in these struggles leads to greater testimony and witness.

Key Themes

- **Continuous Battle Between Flesh and Faith:**

- There is an ongoing conflict between the desires of the flesh and the convictions of faith, where the flesh seeks to undermine and distract from spiritual truth. The author shares how understanding and overcoming this dynamic is crucial for spiritual growth and victory.
- **Power of Persistent Prayer and Intercession:**
- Through detailed narratives, the chapter emphasizes the potency of sustained prayer and intercession, even in the face of great personal cost. The author illustrates how such dedication to prayer can lead to breakthroughs and profound spiritual victories.
- **Role of Personal Conviction:**
- In spiritual warfare, it's not just the faith of those around you that counts, but your own personal declarations and convictions play a crucial role. The author discusses how the turning point in her daughter's struggles came when personal faith and declarations aligned with communal prayer efforts.
- **Impact of Faith on Family Dynamics:**
- The chapter describes how the author's family dynamics were transformed by their collective and individual faith struggles. This transformation underscores the idea that faith challenges, while difficult, can lead to a deeper familial bond and spiritual resilience.
- **Endurance Through Christ's Strength:**

- Drawing on the apostle Paul's words, the author reinforces that believers can endure any challenge through the strength Christ provides. This divine empowerment is central to overcoming the lies and attacks of the enemy.

Conclusion

In summary, "A Wrestling" portrays the relentless struggle between doubt and divine assurance, detailing how believers can emerge victorious through steadfast faith and the power of prayer. The chapter encourages readers to embrace their spiritual battles as opportunities for growth, assuring them of God's faithful presence and the eventual joy that follows enduring faith.

CHAPTER 5

TESTINGS

Bible Verse

"When you pass through the waters, I will be with you; and through the rivers, they shall not overflow you. When you walk through the fire, you shall not be burned, nor shall the flame scorch you." —Isaiah 43:2 (NKJV)

Introduction

This chapter discusses the inevitable challenges and tests of faith that believers face, emphasizing that these moments are opportunities for spiritual growth and deeper reliance on God. Through scriptural examples and personal insights, the author illustrates how God uses these trials to strengthen our faith and prepare us for greater works.

Word of Wisdom

"It is not you working; it is the power of Jesus working through you." Judy Jacobs

Main Theme

The central theme of this chapter is that spiritual testings are not merely obstacles but essential parts of a believer's journey, designed to fortify faith and demonstrate God's faithfulness.

Key Points

- Spiritual testings are a common experience for all believers, designed to strengthen faith.
- Jesus intercedes on our behalf during our trials, as He did for Peter.
- We are empowered by Jesus to overcome the lies and challenges posed by the enemy.
- Our trials are confirmation of our purpose and calling.
- Believers are called to live in spiritual authority over earthly challenges.
- True faith involves active engagement in the world, carrying the message of Christ to all.

Key Themes

- **Intercession and Support During Trials:** Jesus' intercession for Peter before his denial is highlighted as an example of divine support during testings. This shows that while believers will face trials, they are not alone; Christ is actively interceding and ensuring that their faith does not fail.
- **Empowerment Through Weakness:** The chapter stresses that believers are most empowered when they acknowledge their weaknesses, allowing Christ's strength to manifest in them. This paradoxical power is crucial for overcoming the lies and attacks of the enemy during testings.
- **The Anointing Attracts Attacks:** The author discusses the concept that being anointed and called by God often results in increased spiritual attacks. However, these are not signs of failure but confirmations of God's calling and should be seen as opportunities to demonstrate faith.
- **Living in Victory and Authority:** Believers are encouraged to live in the victory and authority that Jesus has given them, which allows them to transcend earthly troubles. This empowerment is a recurring theme that underscores the believer's call to overcome the world as Jesus did.
- **Engagement with the World as a Faith Mission:** Drawing from Jesus' life and commands, the author urges believers not to isolate themselves but to actively

engage with the world. This engagement is not just about spreading the gospel but also about demonstrating the power of living faith in everyday situations.

Conclusion

In conclusion, "Testings" reaffirms that trials and challenges are not only inevitable but are divinely purposed to strengthen believers' faith and prepare them for greater spiritual tasks. The chapter encourages readers to view their trials through the lens of victory and divine empowerment, ensuring that they emerge stronger and more equipped to fulfill their God-given destinies.

CHAPTER 6

NO FRETTING

Bible Verse

"For the joy set before him he endured the cross, scorning its shame, and sat down at the right hand of the throne of God." —Hebrews 12:2 (NIV)

Introduction

This chapter delves into the detrimental effects of worry and emphasizes the importance of facing tests of faith with joy and perseverance. Drawing from biblical examples and personal experiences, the author argues that worry is counterproductive and faith is the key to overcoming life's trials.

Word of Wisdom

"Worry won't change anything. If it would, then let's dedicate the next month to just constantly worrying and then be-

*lieve all of our problems will be solved.
That is not how it works." Judy Jacobs*

Main Theme

The main theme explores the futility of fretting and the power of trusting God through trials, encouraging believers to replace worry with faith and to embrace testing as an opportunity for spiritual growth.

Key Points

- Worrying about things outside our control is contrary to our identity as children of God.
- Jesus explicitly instructs not to fret because it leads to physical and emotional troubles.
- Job's experiences show that what we fear can manifest, highlighting the power of our thoughts.
- James teaches that trials should be met with joy as they develop perseverance and maturity.
- The testing of our faith is inevitable but serves a higher purpose in our spiritual growth.
- Faith and testimony can sustain us through the most challenging tests.

Key Themes

- **Detrimental Effects of Worry:** The author notes that worry can lead to severe health issues and spiritual disconnect. Stressing about the uncontrollable not only harms us physically and emotionally but also hampers our relationship with God.
- **Biblical Encouragement to Reject Worry:** Scriptures like Job 3:25 and Proverbs 18:21 are used to illustrate the negative consequences of giving in to fear and worry. These examples are meant to teach readers that their words and thoughts have power, and they should guard them to foster faith rather than fear.
- **Opportunity in Trials:** Drawing from James 1:2-4, the author reframes trials as opportunities to develop perseverance and spiritual maturity. This perspective encourages believers to face difficulties with a positive outlook, seeing them as necessary for growth.
- **Personal Testimony of Overcoming Worry:** The author shares personal stories of fasting and praying for her daughter, illustrating how facing these challenges without fretting strengthened her faith. These narratives are intended to show that personal and observed experiences can reinforce trust in God's promises.
- **Influence of Faithful Witness:** The passage discusses the communal aspect of faith, where the perseverance of others in the face of trials serves as an encouragement to the individual believer.

It emphasizes that we are part of a larger community of faith that supports and uplifts each other through testimonies and shared experiences.

Conclusion

In conclusion, "No Fretting" calls believers to embrace the tests of their faith with a joyful and confident heart, trusting in God's provision and timing. By focusing on God's promises and the supportive community of faith, believers can navigate their trials without worry, knowing that their faith will lead to spiritual maturity and deeper communion with God.

ROOTED AND GROUNDED

Bible Verse

"But I have pleaded in prayer for you, Simon, that your faith should not fail. So when you have repented and turned to me again, strengthen your brothers." —Luke 22:32 (NLT)

Introduction

This chapter encourages believers to remain steadfast and resilient in their faith, especially during tests and trials. Drawing from biblical examples and personal experiences, the author emphasizes the importance of being rooted and grounded in faith, allowing believers to stand unmovable in the face of challenges.

Word of Wisdom

"It is not by might or by power, but by His Spirit" through our child-like trust in Him. Judy Jacobs

Main Theme

The central theme is the cultivation of a deep, unshakable faith that withstands life's trials through divine strength and guidance, demonstrating the transformative power of trusting God in all circumstances.

Key Points

• Being rooted in faith means standing firm during spiritual and personal trials.

• Child-like faith is crucial, trusting God as a child trusts a loving parent.

• Spiritual battles require the full armor of God to protect and strengthen believers.

• Facing trials is not just about survival but about using these experiences to aid others.

• True faith involves both believing in God's promises and actively engaging in spiritual practices.

Key Themes

- **Importance of Child-like Faith:** The author compares faith to the trust a child places in a parent, highlighting that believers should have unquestioning faith in God's promises. This type of faith is foundational and enables believers to face life's challenges without doubt or fear.
- **Spiritual Resilience in Trials:** Trials are not merely obstacles but opportunities to demonstrate the strength of one's faith.

The author uses the metaphor of being rooted and grounded to describe a faith that is stable and enduring, no matter the external pressures.

- **Armor for Spiritual Warfare:** Drawing from Ephesians 6:12, the chapter details the necessity of putting on spiritual armor daily. This preparation is crucial not only for personal battles but also for protecting and preserving relationships, such as marriage, during spiritual warfare.
- **Role of Testing in Spiritual Growth:** Tests of faith are not punishments but are permitted by God to develop perseverance, character, and deeper faith. The author reassures readers that facing these tests with the right attitude can lead to spiritual maturity and completeness.
- **Empowerment Through Divine Assistance:** The chapter reinforces that believers are not alone in their struggles; they are empowered by God's Spirit. This divine empowerment enables them to overcome any challenge and achieve what seems impossible by human standards.

Conclusion

"Rooted and Grounded" underscores the power of a steadfast faith that does not waver under pressure but grows stronger through trials. The chapter calls on believers to deepen their reliance on God, embracing trials as divine opportunities for growth and witness, ensuring they remain firm in their faith through life's inevitable challenges.

CHAPTER 8
CEASELESS PRAYER

Bible Verse
"Pray without ceasing." — 1 Thessalonians 5:17
(NKJV)

Introduction

This chapter underscores the power of constant, heartfelt prayer, emphasizing that prayer should be as natural and on-going as conversation with a close friend. Through personal anecdotes and biblical teachings, the author encourages believers to engage in ceaseless, faith-filled prayer as a way of life.

Word of Wisdom

"Prayer in its simplest form is just talking to God like you would talk to your best friend." Judy Jacobs

Main Theme

The main theme focuses on the transformative power of continuous prayer in a believer's life, highlighting how such prayer fosters a deeper relationship with God and enables believers to navigate life's challenges with divine support.

Key Points

• Continuous prayer is a fundamental aspect of a believer's life, vital for maintaining spiritual vitality.

• Jesus and the scriptures emphasize the necessity and expectation of ceaseless prayer.

• True prayer is a simple, conversational engagement with God, not bound by formality.

• The effects of prayer are not limited to spiritual growth but extend to fulfilling God's purposes on Earth.

• Persistent prayer cultivates an environment where miracles and divine interventions are possible.

• Prayer should be approached as an ongoing dialogue, involving both speaking and listening.

Key Themes

- **Nature of Prayer as Continuous Communication:** The chapter portrays prayer not as a sporadic or formal ritual but as continuous, open communication with God, akin to breathing. This approach demystifies prayer, making it more accessible and integral to daily life, encouraging believers to engage with God throughout their day.

- **Impact of Prayer on Spiritual Resilience:** By illustrating prayer as an essential tool for spiritual resilience, the author connects the practice of ceaseless prayer with the ability to withstand life's trials. This constant communication with God builds trust and strength, enabling believers to overcome any obstacle with divine backing.
- **Conversational Prayer versus Formal Prayer:** The author advocates for a conversational approach to prayer, which fosters a more personal and profound connection with God. This method breaks down barriers that may prevent believers from engaging in prayer, promoting a more relaxed and effective communication style.
- **Role of Prayer in Achieving God's Purpose:** Prayer is depicted not only as a means of personal support but as a crucial activity in fulfilling God's kingdom purposes on Earth. Through prayer, believers can participate in God's work, influencing outcomes and bringing about change in line with divine will.
- **Listening as a Component of Prayer:** Emphasizing the importance of listening in prayer, the chapter advises believers to balance their petitions with silence, allowing space for God to speak. This practice enriches the prayer experience, ensuring it is a true dialogue rather than a one-sided conversation.

Conclusion

"Ceaseless Prayer" calls on believers to integrate prayer into every aspect of their lives, advocating for a dynamic and ongoing dialogue with God that is natural and unceasing. This approach empowers believers to live in constant communion with God, ensuring they are spiritually equipped to face any situation with confidence and grace.

CHAPTER 9
YOUR ARSENAL

Bible Verse

"The effectual fervent prayer of a righteous man availeth much." — James 5:16 (KJV)

Introduction

In this chapter, the author shares a powerful testimony about the life-saving power of ceaseless prayer, recounting a specific incident in her husband's life. While on a mission trip to the Philippines, he experienced a near-death situation, but through fervent prayer—especially his mother's intercession—he was miraculously saved. The chapter encourages believers to view prayer as a constant, life-sustaining force that can bring forth miracles and divine intervention in times of need.

Word of Wisdom

"Think of the concept of prayer as breath in your lungs and blood from your

heart. The blood flows and the breath in our lungs continues without ceasing. In the same way, we should let prayer be a ceaseless flowing from one moment to the next." Judy Jacobs

Main Theme

The chapter illustrates the power of persistent prayer, focusing on how a mother's fervent intercession brought her son back from the brink of death. Through this personal testimony, the author emphasizes the importance of having an "arsenal" of prayer, always ready to activate in times of crisis. The story serves as a reminder that prayer is not a last resort but a vital and constant connection with God that leads to miraculous outcomes.

Key Points

• Ceaseless prayer can bring forth miracles, even in the most dire circumstances.

• Specific words of prophecy can serve as warnings or preparations for trials ahead.

• God often awakens intercessors to pray, even when they are not aware of the full circumstances.

• Prayer should be viewed as a continual life force, just like breathing or the flow of blood.

• God responds to the fervent prayers of righteous people, even when we cannot see the immediate results.

• Diligent seeking in prayer positions believers for divine miracles and protection.

Key Themes

- **The Power of Prophetic Prayer:** Dr. Rutland's prayer over Jamie before the mission trip foretold a future challenge. His words, "be with him, especially when he gets separated from the rest of the group," prepared Jamie for the trial ahead, though its full meaning wasn't clear at the time. Prophetic prayer can serve as both guidance and a shield.
- **A Mother's Ceaseless Intercession:** Jamie's mother exemplifies the role of a persistent intercessor. When she sensed her son was in danger, she fervently prayed, even crawling into her closet in the middle of the night. Her unwavering faith and determination were instrumental in saving her son's life.
- **The Life-Sustaining Nature of Prayer:** The author likens prayer to breathing and the flow of blood, emphasizing that it should be continuous and vital to a believer's spiritual life. Prayer is not just an occasional act but a constant, life-sustaining connection to God.
- **God's Perfect Timing and Provision:** Despite being far from home in a third-world hospital, Jamie's recovery was a testament to God's ability to intervene. The presence of intercessors and God's protection provided healing when no other resources were available.

- **Positioning for Miracles:** The chapter closes by encouraging believers to adopt the right position in prayer. God hears and responds to diligent seekers, and miracles are often the result of fervent, faithful intercession. The posture of one's heart and mind in prayer can make all the difference in times of crisis.

Conclusion

Through the testimony of her husband's near-death experience and miraculous recovery, the author stresses the crucial role of prayer in every believer's life. Ceaseless, fervent prayer, like breath or blood, should flow continuously and be an integral part of our spiritual walk. God hears and responds to the prayers of the righteous, and in times of need, miracles will manifest when we persistently seek Him. Let prayer be your greatest weapon in life's spiritual battles.

CHAPTER 10

PRAYER POSTURE

Bible Verse

"Watch and pray, that ye enter not into temptation:
the spirit indeed is willing, but the flesh is weak."
—Matthew 26:41 (KJV)

Introduction

This chapter discusses the significance of maintaining a determined and committed posture in prayer, especially during times of deep spiritual testing. Drawing on biblical narratives and personal experiences, the author illustrates how adopting a physical and spiritual stance of prayer can lead to divine breakthroughs and support.

Word of Wisdom

"There is a posture in prayer that must be taken on when you are praying for a breakthrough. It is an unashamedly

violent posture of determination in your heart, mind, and spirit that things will change." Judy Jacobs

Main Theme

The main theme explores the concept of "prayer posture," which is not just about physical position but a metaphor for the attitude and stance believers must take when engaging in serious prayer—fully committed, focused, and expecting God to move.

Key Points

• Prayer posture is both a physical and spiritual concept that enhances communication with God.

• The intensity of one's prayer posture can determine the outcome of spiritual battles.

• Biblical figures like Jesus and Elijah exemplified powerful prayer postures during crucial moments.

• Maintaining a committed prayer posture can lead to angelic support and divine intervention.

• Every believer has moments that require a "Gethsemane" level of prayer intensity.

• The resolve to remain steadfast in prayer is likened to a pilot's commitment to takeoff—fully committed without turning back.

Key Themes

- **Biblical Examples of Prayer Posture:** Jesus' prayer in Gethsemane and Elijah's posture on Mount Carmel are pivotal examples that highlight the importance of physical and spiritual positioning in prayer. These moments show that how we approach God in prayer can reflect our intensity, desperation, and expectation for Him to act.

- **Spiritual Determination Reflected in Physical Posture:** Adopting a specific prayer posture can symbolize and even enhance a believer's spiritual resolve. Whether it is bowing deeply as Elijah did or falling to the ground as Jesus did, these actions underscore a surrender to God's will and an urgent petition for His intervention.

- **Impact of Committed Prayer on Spiritual Warfare:** The chapter discusses how a committed prayer posture is crucial in spiritual warfare, helping believers to stand firm against the enemy's schemes. Such a posture ensures that believers are not passive but are actively engaging in battle with the assurance of victory.

- **The Role of Angelic Support in Prayer:** By maintaining a steadfast prayer posture, believers can experience supernatural comfort and support, as Jesus did when angels came to minister to Him. This divine assistance is depicted as crucial in moments of extreme spiritual duress.

- **Encouragement to Persist in Prayer Despite Challenges:** The author encourages believers to persist in their prayer efforts despite feeling tired or hopeless, suggesting that breakthroughs often occur just beyond the point of greatest resistance. This persistence is crucial in achieving the victories that God has planned for those who do not give up.

Conclusion

"Prayer Posture" concludes by affirming the power of maintaining a dedicated stance in prayer, both physically and spiritually. The author calls believers to embrace a posture of unwavering faith and commitment, promising that such a stance will lead to profound spiritual victories and fulfillment of God's promises.

CHAPTER 11

BATTLING FEAR

Bible Verse

"For God has not given us a spirit of fear, but of power and of love and of a sound mind." —2 Timothy 1:7 (NKJV)

Introduction

This chapter highlights the personal and spiritual journey of overcoming fear, using the story of Kaylee's battle with fear as a backdrop. It emphasizes the transition from parental guidance to personal responsibility in spiritual warfare, illustrating how one must actively engage in their own deliverance through faith and prayer.

Word of Wisdom

"It matters how you approach God in this season of your life! It matters that you go the extra mile!" Judy Jacobs

Main Theme

The main theme explores the personal fight against fear, emphasizing the importance of individual action, the power of prayer, and the necessity of adopting a proactive spiritual posture to achieve personal breakthrough and deliverance.

Key Points

• Kaylee had to take personal responsibility to fight her battle against fear.

• Parents can provide tools and support but ultimately, the individual must engage in the battle.

• Personal engagement in prayer and worship is crucial for overcoming spiritual challenges.

• This personal battle led to spiritual growth and ministry opportunities for Kaylee and her sister Erica.

• Obedience to God's directives, no matter how challenging, leads to breakthroughs.

Key Themes

- **Personal Responsibility in Spiritual Warfare:**
- The transition from parental support to personal responsibility is critical in spiritual battles. Kaylee's story illustrates that while support is necessary, personal engagement and responsibility are key to overcoming deep-seated fears.
- **Impact of Prayer and Worship:**

- Prayer and worship are portrayed as powerful tools in the battle against fear. By engaging deeply in these spiritual disciplines, Kaylee was able to transform her spiritual environment, leading to personal and communal victories.
- **Influence of Faith on Family Dynamics:**
- The spiritual battles of one family member can influence the entire family. Kaylee's fight against fear not only led to her deliverance but also inspired her sister, leading to a joint ministry that impacts others.
- **Role of Obedience in Overcoming Fear:**
- Obedience to God's will, even when it seems foolish or difficult, is a crucial theme. The narrative shows that radical obedience can ignite faith and bring about miraculous results, changing the course of one's spiritual journey.
- **Demonstration of Faith in Action:**
- Faith is active and demonstrative, not passive or hidden. The chapter underscores that true faith involves visible actions and decisions that reflect a firm trust in God, leading to tangible outcomes in the believer's life.

Conclusion

"Battling Fear" concludes by reinforcing the idea that overcoming fear requires a proactive stance in prayer and faith, personal responsibility, and a readiness to act on God's instructions. The narrative encourages readers to embrace their spiritual battles as opportunities for growth and transformation, ensuring they are equipped with the spiritual tools necessary to achieve victory.

CHAPTER 12

WALKING BY FAITH

Bible Verse

"Noah was a righteous man, the only blameless person living on earth at the time, and he walked in close fellowship with God." —Genesis 6:9 (NLT)

Introduction

This chapter explores the profound commitment and integrity required to walk by faith, using Noah as a prime biblical example. It delves into how faith, aligned with God's will, necessitates continual obedience and how such a lifestyle is essential in a world filled with challenges and corruption.

Word of Wisdom

"The grace of God will get you to the other side of your flood like Noah, your lion's den like Daniel, and your driest season like Elijah." Judy Jacobs

Main Theme

The main theme focuses on the necessity of steadfast faith and obedience in the believer's life, highlighting how such spiritual posture enables one to navigate through life's most challenging circumstances.

Key Points

• Noah exemplified an obedient faith, walking closely with God despite societal corruption.

• God's grace was sufficient for Noah to overcome the catastrophic flood.

• Like Noah, believers today are called to walk in faith amidst moral decay.

• Elijah's faith was similarly impactful, demonstrating that effective prayer stems from a heart aligned with God.

• Walking by faith involves daily commitment and is empowered by God's grace.

• True faith manifests in concrete actions and decisions that align with God's will.

Key Themes

• **Faith in a Corrupt World:** The narrative describes Noah's environment as profoundly corrupt, yet he maintained his integrity and obedience. This sets a precedent for believers today, showing that it is possible to live righteously and walk by faith even when surrounded by widespread moral decay.

- **Grace as the Enabler of Faith:** The grace of God is portrayed as a crucial element that enables believers to endure and overcome great trials. This divine favor is not just a historical concept but a present reality that supports believers in their own "floods" and challenges.
- **Daily Walk and Continual Obedience:** Emphasis is placed on the daily aspect of walking by faith, requiring continual decisions to trust and obey God. This daily commitment is what builds a life of faith that is able to withstand and overcome great trials.
- **Practical Faith in Biblical Characters:** The chapter points out that biblical figures like Noah and Elijah were ordinary humans who achieved extraordinary feats through faith. This demystifies the concept of faith, making it accessible and achievable for every believer.
- **Impact of Faithful Living:** By living faithfully, believers set a standard and have a profound impact on their surroundings. Noah's life not only preserved his family but essentially reset the course of human history, illustrating the vast potential of a life lived in obedient faith.

Conclusion

"Walking by Faith" encourages believers to adopt a lifestyle of unwavering faith and obedience, taking inspiration from biblical examples like Noah and Elijah. It calls for a commitment to live daily in close fellowship with God, utilizing His grace to overcome any of life's challenges, and making faith a practical, everyday reality.

CHAPTER 13

ON TOES AND KNEES

Bible Verse

"Elijah was a man with a nature like ours, and he prayed earnestly that it would not rain, and it did not rain on the land for three years and six months." —James 5:17 (NKJV)

Introduction

This chapter illustrates the dynamic and proactive nature of faith, using Elijah's dramatic encounter on Mount Carmel as a model. It emphasizes the necessity of adopting both a physical and spiritual posture of determination and focus in prayer, especially when contending for a breakthrough.

Word of Wisdom

"When you see faith, you have to declare faith." Judy Jacobs

Main Theme

The main theme discusses the relentless and persistent nature of faith that doesn't merely wait passively but actively engages in spiritual battles, drawing parallels between biblical accounts and practical applications for modern believers.

Key Points

• Faith requires constant vigilance and spiritual readiness.

• Elijah's prayer on Mount Carmel serves as a profound example of active faith.

• True faith involves repeated actions and checks, as shown by Elijah sending his servant to look for rain.

• Spiritual victories are often preceded by intense spiritual warfare.

• Faith sees beyond the physical to the assurance of God's promises.

• Persistent faith can lead to miraculous outcomes, changing natural circumstances.

Key Themes

• **Engaged and Active Faith:** The chapter stresses the importance of being engaged in one's faith journey, not passively but actively, by being on one's toes and knees. This posture indicates readiness to move as directed by God and to kneel in submission and earnest prayer.

- **Persistence in Prayer:** Elijah's example of sending his servant seven times to look for signs of rain illustrates the biblical principle of persistent, expectant prayer. This persistence is crucial for believers who are contending for their own breakthroughs and miracles.
- **The Power of Prophetic Action:** Elijah's actions on Mount Carmel demonstrate that faith sometimes requires prophetic gestures that may seem foolish to onlookers but are powerful acts of obedience to God's instructions.
- **The Role of Physical Posture in Spiritual Battles:** Adopting a specific physical posture, like Elijah's birthing position, can symbolize and intensify one's spiritual focus and determination. This chapter encourages believers to find their own posture of faith that aids their concentration and spiritual intensity.
- **Victory Through Obedience:** The ultimate outcome of Elijah's faith and obedience was not just rain but a demonstration of God's supremacy to Israel. This teaches that obedience to God's commands can lead to victories that are both personal and corporate, impacting a wider community.

Conclusion

"On Toes and Knees" concludes by reaffirming the active and engaged nature of biblical faith. It calls believers to a life of constant readiness and deep communion with God, where faith is not static but moves with the promptings of the Holy Spirit. Through persistent prayer and unwavering focus, believers are equipped to face any challenge and see God's power manifested in their lives.

CHAPTER 14

BIG PRAYERS, BIG ANSWERS

Bible Verse

"Jesus looked at them and said, 'With man this is impossible, but with God all things are possible.'"
—Matthew 19:26 (NIV)

Introduction

This chapter encourages believers to approach God with grand expectations, asserting that God responds generously to bold, faith-filled prayers. It uses personal anecdotes to illustrate how daring to pray ambitiously can lead to remarkable divine responses.

Word of Wisdom

"God is not stingy. He always gives from His abundance, not ours." Judy Jacobs

Main Theme

The theme of this chapter centers on the power of praying expansive prayers and expecting significant answers from God. It challenges believers to elevate their prayer life by trusting in the supernatural capabilities of God rather than being confined by their natural circumstances.

Key Points

• God delights in answering big prayers that reflect deep faith and trust in His supernatural power.

• Personal testimony highlights a significant answer to prayer regarding office space, underscoring God's provision.

• Challenges and discomfort can serve as divine catalysts pushing believers towards greater faith and reliance on God.

• The importance of maintaining a posture of expectancy and readiness to receive God's blessings.

• Encourages believers to embrace moments of divine push to expand their territories and capacities.

Key Themes

• **The Nature of God's Generosity:** The chapter emphasizes that God's nature is to be abundantly generous, providing beyond human expectations or calculations. This attribute of God encourages believers to pray without reservations, trusting that

God will respond in a manner that reflects His boundless grace and power.

- **Faith as a Catalyst for Divine Action:** It illustrates that audacious faith, expressed through bold prayers, activates divine responses that transcend normal expectations. The narrative encourages believers to not only ask for what they need but to dare to ask for what seems impossible, highlighting that such faith pleases God and often leads to miraculous outcomes.

- **Practical Implications of Faithful Prayers:** Using personal stories, the chapter shows how faith is not just a spiritual concept but has practical implications, leading to real-life miracles and testimonies that can inspire and encourage others in their faith journey.

- **Encouragement in Times of Doubt:** Acknowledges that even strong believers can experience moments of doubt or financial impossibility. It reassures that these moments are opportunities for God to demonstrate His faithfulness and power, urging believers to remain steadfast in their expectations of God's action.

- **The Role of Divine Timing:** Discusses the concept of divine timing in the manifestation of prayer answers, encouraging patience and persistent faith while waiting for God's timing, which often comes just when believers are pushed beyond their comfort zones.

Conclusion

"Big Prayers, Big Answers" concludes by reinforcing the message that God is not limited by human constraints and that He delights in exceeding the expectations of His children. It invites believers to transform their prayer life by consistently practicing faith that believes for and expects big answers, assuring them of God's readiness to act mightily on their behalf.

CHAPTER 15

GREAT AND MIGHTY

Bible Verse

"Call to me and I will answer you and tell you great and hidden things that you have not known." — Jeremiah 33:3 (ESV)

Introduction

This chapter is a motivational call to readers facing uncertainties and discomfort, encouraging them to recognize these feelings as precursors to divine elevation and breakthroughs. It underscores the theme that with great faith come great results.

Word of Wisdom

"You were made for greatness, born for this very moment, and you are getting ready to fly." Judy Jacobs

Main Theme

The main theme focuses on embracing the divine timing and provision that come with big visions and prayers. It reassures readers that God is preparing them for significant achievements and encourages them to keep faith despite financial or spiritual constraints.

Key Points

• Challenges and discomfort are often signs that God is preparing you for greater things.

• Faith should not be limited by current resources or circumstances.

• Visionaries often face financial constraints that test their faith.

• The importance of praying big prayers with the expectation of big results.

• Faith actions often precede financial provision and are rewarded by God.

Key Themes

• **Understanding Discomfort as Divine Setup** The chapter suggests that discomfort and restlessness can be indicators of imminent divine action. It encourages believers to see these moments as opportunities for growth and preparation for what God is about to do in their lives, urging them to maintain their faith.

- **Vision Beyond Resources:** It presents a narrative that faith and vision often transcend current resources, and divine provision follows bold steps taken in obedience to God. This theme is illustrated through personal stories where financial limitations did not hinder the fulfillment of God's promises.
- **Role of Vision in Ministry Growth:** The chapter recounts how a vision for ministry expansion led to significant steps of faith, despite financial constraints. It shows how envisioning larger projects can lead to actual possession and realization of those projects, provided there is steadfast faith.
- **Encouragement to Persist in Faith:** Believers are encouraged to persist in their faith even when immediate circumstances seem daunting. The chapter emphasizes that spiritual persistence can lead to breakthroughs and that discomfort should be seen as a setup for God's greater plans.
- **Empowerment Through Big Prayers:** It concludes by empowering readers to pray ambitiously and to expect miracles, reinforcing that God delights in fulfilling the grand visions He plants within His followers. This ties into the overarching message that believers are destined for greatness and equipped for significant achievements.

Conclusion

"Great and Mighty" concludes by affirming that

believers are created for significant purposes and that current struggles or discomforts are merely preparations for greater achievements. It encourages readers to embrace their divine assignments with faith, expecting that God will enable them to achieve extraordinary things for His glory.

CHAPTER 16

THAT DAY

Bible Verse
"Ask of me, and I will make the nations your
inheritance, the ends of the earth your possession."
—Psalm 2:8 (NIV)

Introduction

This chapter explores the transformative power of prayer in overcoming logistical and spiritual challenges, inspired by the global changes following the 9/11 attacks. It recounts personal family anecdotes to illustrate how faith and prayer can lead to miraculous provisions.

Word of Wisdom

"You may want to watch what you pray for, because you just might get it!"
Judy Jacobs

Main Theme

The main theme of this chapter is about trusting in divine provision during times of transition and crisis. It highlights how big prayers can lead to significant changes in life and ministry, encouraging a mindset that embraces God's abundant blessings.

Key Points

• The 9/11 attacks brought unprecedented changes and challenges globally.

• Personal story of family's adjustment, highlighting the emotional impact on children.

• Decision to acquire a bus for safer, more comfortable family travel.

• Transition from small office space to a larger facility due to growing ministry needs.

• Emphasis on the power of persistent, faith-driven prayers.

Key Themes

- **Impact of Global Crises on Personal Faith:** The aftermath of 9/11 led to increased security measures that affected everyone, including the author's family. This section reflects on how global events can prompt personal re-evaluation of faith and reliance on God.
- **Prayer as a Tool for Overcoming Logistical Challenges:** Through the story of needing a new bus, the chapter

illustrates how prayer is not just spiritual but practically applicable in solving daily challenges, encouraging believers to trust God for big things.

- **Visionary Thinking and Divine Provision:** It discusses how visionary thinking, like envisaging a larger office space, can align with God's provisions. This theme encourages readers to not limit their prayers or visions by their current resources.
- **The Role of Prayer in Ministry Expansion:** This section details the journey from praying for immediate needs to envisioning larger ministry expansions, showing how prayer underpins every step of faith and ministry growth.
- **Mentorship as a Divine Calling:** The call to establish a women's mentoring institute illustrates how God can introduce completely new directions for our lives and ministries, and how these calls require obedience and faith.

Conclusion

"That Day" closes with a powerful affirmation of God's capacity to answer prayers in a monumental way, urging readers to not only believe in the possibility of divine answers but to actively seek them with expectancy. It serves as a reminder that God's plans often exceed our own and come with the promise of His unfailing support.

CHAPTER 17

MORE BIG PRAYERS ANSWERED

Bible Verse

"Call to me and I will answer you and tell you great and unsearchable things you do not know." — Jeremiah 33:3 (NIV)

Introduction

This chapter recounts the author's experience of trusting in God's provision for a seemingly impossible financial situation, illustrating how faith and obedience can lead to miraculous outcomes in the acquisition of necessary property for ministry expansion.

Word of Wisdom

"It is true that God does speak the loudest in bathtubs and showers." Judy Jacobs

Main Theme

The theme centers on the power of prayer, specifically the impact of persistent and faith-filled prayers on achieving significant breakthroughs in life and ministry.

Key Points

• Prayed for the right bus and building at an affordable price.

• Experienced divine confirmation to offer a seemingly low amount for a highly valued property.

• Encountered a realtor and a property owner receptive to their faith-driven offer.

• Received the property at a miraculous price, far below the asking value.

• Affirmed the importance of bold, faith-filled prayers in achieving God's provision.

Key Themes

- **Faith in Financial Negotiations:** Despite the high market value of the desired property, the author, guided by divine insight, boldly proposed a significantly lower offer. This theme explores the intersection of faith and financial negotiations, emphasizing that with God, financial norms can be defied.
- **Experiencing God's Favor in Transactions:** The property owner's surprising acceptance of the low offer and

his additional financial concessions demonstrate how divine favor can operate in practical aspects of life, such as real estate transactions.

- **The Role of Vision in Prayer:** Sharing a God-given vision with others played a crucial role in the negotiation process, showing that articulating a clear and divinely inspired vision can influence outcomes and align others with one's spiritual objectives.

- **Testimony as a Tool for Encouragement:** The author uses personal testimony to encourage others to trust in God's provision. This theme underscores the power of sharing testimonies to build faith and inspire prayer in others.

- **Perseverance in Prayer:** The chapter illustrates the necessity of persistent and bold prayers, especially when facing daunting challenges. It reinforces the concept that perseverance in prayer can lead to extraordinary results beyond human expectations.

Conclusion

"More Big Prayers Answered" is a testament to the efficacy of praying with expectation and boldness, demonstrating that God is not limited by human constraints and often responds in ways that exceed our imaginations. This narrative encourages readers to trust in God's timing and provision, reinforcing the biblical principle that nothing is too hard for God.

CHAPTER 18

ALREADY HAPPENED

Bible Verse

"[God] calleth those things which be not as though they were." —Romans 4:17 (KJV)

Introduction

This chapter delves into the profound truth that God's responses to our prayers are established in the spiritual realm even before we see their manifestations in the physical. It explores the faith journey of trusting in God's timing and provision through the story of a significant financial contribution made in faith.

Word of Wisdom

"God sees the end from the beginning, and what He has ordained has already happened in the spiritual realm; we are

just waiting for the manifestation on earth." Judy Jacobs

Main Theme

The theme emphasizes the reality of spiritual provision and the manifestation of prayers that have already been answered in the spiritual realm, as believers wait for their physical realization.

Key Points

• Participated in a significant offering at a church conference despite financial constraints.

• Experienced initial doubts and fears about the financial commitment made.

• Received a miraculous financial gift shortly after making a significant faith-based decision.

• Reinforced the belief that God pre-ordains answers to prayers in the spiritual realm.

• Demonstrated the power of faith and obedience in financial stewardship.

Key Themes

• **Trusting in Prophetic Promptings:**
The decision to donate a substantial sum
was based on a strong spiritual prompting,
illustrating the importance of being
responsive to the Holy Spirit's guidance

even when it seems contrary to human logic.

- **Miraculous Provision Following Obedience:** The miraculous receipt of a significant sum shortly after the act of obedience highlights that God honors faith and bold actions, reinforcing the principle that God provides supernaturally for the needs aligned with His purposes.
- **Spiritual Realities Preceding Physical Manifestations:** The concept that God's answers exist in the spiritual realm before they are evident in the physical is explored, encouraging believers to have faith in the unseen workings of God in response to their prayers.
- **The Impact of Faithful Stewardship:** This narrative underscores the importance of faithful stewardship and sacrificial giving as acts of worship and trust in God, which lead to divine multiplication and provision.
- **Learning to Trust in Divine Timing:** The story conveys a lesson on the importance of divine timing, illustrating that God's schedule for answering prayers often surpasses human expectations and leads to greater outcomes than anticipated.

Conclusion

"Already Happened" serves as a powerful testimony to the fact that God is always working behind the scenes. It encourages believers to maintain their faith and commitment, assuring them that their prayers are not in vain and that God's responses are orchestrated for the perfect timing to maximize their impact and testimony.

CHAPTER 19

HAPPY BIRTHDAY!

Bible Verse

"All things work together for good to those who love God, to those who are the called according to His purpose." —
Romans 8:28 (NKJV)

Introduction

This chapter recounts the incredible journey of faith and the manifestation of God's promises through substantial financial blessings following significant acts of obedience and big prayers by the author and her family.

Word of Wisdom

"If you will pray big prayers, you will get big answers!" Judy Jacobs

Main Theme

The chapter illustrates the profound impact of trusting in God's provision, highlighting the miraculous financial support received for ministry work as a result of fervent and faith-filled prayers.

Key Points

• Ministered at a venue despite being sick, relying on God's strength.

• Received a $100,000 seed from the venue's hosts who shared a similar vision.

• Celebrated a milestone birthday with surprise gifts totaling $100,000 in donations.

• These donations significantly contributed towards building a ministry center debt-free.

• Witnessed the birth of a church that meets broad community needs.

Key Themes

- **Power of Obedience and Generosity:** Despite challenges, the author and her husband's obedience to God's prompting to sow financially into other ministries led to unexpected financial blessings that supported their own ministry's goals.
- **Significance of Community and Shared Vision:** The support from like-minded believers not only affirmed the author's ministry vision but also propelled them toward achieving significant

milestones, demonstrating the power of collective faith and shared purpose.

- **Impact of Faithful Stewardship:** The story highlights how faithful stewardship and strategic giving can lead to divine multiplication of resources, underscoring the principle that God rewards faith and obedience with abundance.
- **Celebration as a Catalyst for Blessing:** The author's milestone birthday became a moment of unexpected joy and provision, showing how God uses significant occasions to deliver blessings and confirm His promises.
- **Expansion Beyond Initial Expectations:** What began as a vision for a ministry building expanded to include a thriving church, illustrating how God's plans often exceed our initial dreams and expectations.

Conclusion

"Happy Birthday!" serves as a testimony to the efficacy of "big prayers" which led to "big answers." It encourages readers to trust in God's timing and provision, and to expect miracles on the path of obedience and faith. The narrative reassures that God is always working behind the scenes, preparing to unleash blessings that align with His divine purpose for our lives.

BIG FAITH

Bible Verse

"Because of your faith, it will happen." — Matthew 9:29 (NLT)

Introduction

"Big Faith" explores the necessity of having a robust faith to invoke God's action, emphasizing the significance of expanding one's spiritual capacity through consistent refinement and personal growth.

Word of Wisdom

"God sees the end from the beginning, calling things that are not as though they were, demanding our faith to align with His vision." Judy Jacobs

Main Theme

This chapter underlines the importance of having a faith that is capable of embracing and realizing God's grand plans, requiring believers to stretch beyond their current limits and trust in divine adjustments.

Key Points

• Big prayers are predicated on having a substantial faith that anticipates and believes in remarkable outcomes.

• Understanding and embracing the concept of "tweaking" and "pruning" as necessary for growth and better alignment with God's will.

• The process of spiritual refinement is ongoing and encompasses every aspect of a believer's life.

• Challenges and adjustments are viewed as opportunities for development rather than obstacles.

• True faith involves a dynamic relationship with God, characterized by continual learning and adaptation.

Key Themes

• **Spiritual Adjustment and Refinement:** God's tweaking of our lives involves adjusting our attitudes, improving our gifts, and refining our character to better reflect His glory. This process is continual and requires an open heart willing to undergo transformation for greater spiritual efficacy.

- **Faith as a Catalyst for Miraculous Outcomes:** By stretching our faith and trusting in God's supernatural abilities, we open ourselves to witnessing extraordinary happenings. Faith is not just believing in the possible but also in the seemingly impossible, which God turns into reality.
- **Role of Character and Integrity in Faith:** As believers positioned to influence the world, maintaining integrity and a righteous character is crucial. These traits ensure that our faith and actions align with God's expectations and effectively draw others towards Him.
- **The Comfort in Divine Knowledge and Plans:** Despite the challenges of being under God's intensive scrutiny, there is comfort in knowing that He is intimately familiar with our nature and orchestrates our lives for the ultimate good, even when His methods are beyond our understanding.
- **Living in Expectation of God's Continuous Work:** The chapter encourages living in a state of expectation for God's interventions, which are often surprising and surpass our expectations. As we align our desires with His will, God not only meets but also exceeds the visions we have for our lives.

Conclusion

"Big Faith" serves as a compelling reminder that

the size of our faith directly influences the magnitude of God's responses. It calls on believers to expand their spiritual horizons, embrace divine adjustments, and anticipate God's mighty acts, which manifest profoundly in lives grounded in faith and obedience.

CHAPTER 21

TWEAKING

Bible Verse

"We...are being transformed into the same image from glory to glory, just as by the Spirit of the Lord." — 2 Corinthians 3:18 (NKJV)

Introduction

The chapter "Tweaking" uses the metaphor of refining a musical recording to explore the concept of God's continual refinement of our lives, aiming for perfection in our spiritual journey.

Word of Wisdom

"In God's studio, every adjustment is made with divine precision, aiming for a masterpiece reflective of His perfect will."
Judy Jacobs

Main Theme

This chapter emphasizes the ongoing process of spiritual 'tweaking' where God meticulously shapes and adjusts our character and actions to align more closely with His will.

Key Points

• Tweaking involves making precise adjustments to improve overall performance, akin to refining a vocal track in a recording studio.

• Just as a recording engineer listens for flaws, God notices areas in our lives that require correction and enhancement.

• The discomfort during tweaking is a necessary part of growth, leading to a more harmonious spiritual life.

• Our willingness to undergo God's tweaking process is crucial for our spiritual development and effectiveness.

• The result of divine tweaking is a life that resonates more clearly with God's purpose and design.

Key Themes

- **Spiritual Refinement as Divine Tweaking:** God's process of tweaking in our lives is compared to a producer refining a vocal performance, where small adjustments lead to significantly better outcomes. This divine intervention is essential for removing spiritual imperfections and enhancing our strengths.

- **The Role of Prayer in Spiritual Adjustment:** Prayer is the medium through which we seek God's guidance on what adjustments are needed, allowing us to embrace the changes He proposes. It's a space for honest reflection and a willingness to change according to God's directives.

- **Challenges as Opportunities for Growth:** Periods of intense challenge or discomfort are viewed as opportunities for significant spiritual growth. These moments, while difficult, are when God's tweaking is most active, aiming to strengthen our faith and character.

- **The Importance of Divine Alignment:** The ultimate goal of tweaking is to ensure our lives are in full alignment with God's will. This alignment improves our spiritual resonance and impacts, ensuring we fulfill our divine purpose effectively.

- **Continuous Process of Transformation:** Transformation through tweaking is not a one-time event but a continuous journey of spiritual evolution. As we grow closer to God, our understanding deepens, and our capacity to embody His qualities expands.

Conclusion

"Tweaking" presents a powerful analogy of God's meticulous work in our lives, urging us to remain open to His guidance and corrections. The chapter calls for embracing the sometimes uncomfortable but always fruitful process of divine refinement, ensuring our spiritual growth and readiness to fulfill God's purposes.

CHAPTER 22

PRUNING

Bible Verse

"Every branch in Me that does not bear fruit, He takes away; and every branch that bears fruit, He prunes it so that it may bear more fruit." — John 15:2 (NASB)

Introduction

The chapter "Pruning" discusses the essential spiritual discipline of pruning, likening it to horticultural practices that promote growth and health. It emphasizes the necessity of undergoing divine pruning to enhance spiritual vitality and productivity.

Word of Wisdom

"Pruning is not punishment; it is preparation for greater things. Welcome it, for it leads to abundant life." Judy Jacobs

Main Theme

This chapter elaborates on the metaphor of pruning as a divine process that removes spiritual deadweight and unnecessary distractions, enabling believers to flourish in their faith and produce more fruit.

Key Points

• Pruning is vital for removing unproductive elements in our lives, allowing for new growth and greater fruitfulness.

• Just as in gardening, spiritual pruning involves thinning, topping, raising, and reduction to improve overall health and function.

• Experienced pruning leads to the best outcomes, ensuring that growth is directed and beneficial.

• Poor or inexperienced pruning can cause harm, underscoring the importance of trusting God, the skilled pruner.

• Pruning occurs at key moments, often before new growth cycles, preparing us for what God has planned next.

Key Themes

• **Purpose and Benefits of Pruning:**
Pruning is designed to remove aspects of our lives that hinder spiritual growth, such as dead or unproductive habits, to make way for a healthier spiritual life. This process is crucial for maintaining spiritual

vitality and ensuring we are aligned with God's purposes.

- **Methods and Timing of Pruning:** Different pruning techniques such as thinning and topping are used depending on the specific needs of the plant, analogous to how God uniquely shapes each believer's life. Timing is critical, as pruning should occur when it is most beneficial for growth, reflecting the strategic timing of God's interventions in our lives.

- **Impact of Skilled vs. Unskilled Pruning:** The skill of the pruner affects the outcome, highlighting the importance of submitting to God's experienced hands rather than resisting His corrections. Trusting God's expertise ensures that pruning leads to flourishing rather than harm.

- **Spiritual Growth through Difficult Processes:** While pruning can be uncomfortable and challenging, it is essential for bearing more fruit and achieving a greater resemblance to Christ. Believers are encouraged to embrace these periods of cutting away with faith that they will lead to increased spiritual abundance.

- **The Final Outcome of Divine Pruning:** The ultimate goal of pruning is to produce a bountiful, beautiful display of spiritual fruit that glorifies God. Each cut and adjustment made by our divine gardener is aimed at creating a masterpiece

of faith and obedience that shines brightly
in the world.

Conclusion

"Pruning" offers profound insights into the
necessary discomforts of spiritual growth,
encouraging believers to trust in God's purposeful
and loving modifications. Through the metaphor of
pruning, readers are invited to see life's challenges
as opportunities for transformation and renewal,
ultimately leading to a more fruitful and fulfilled
spiritual journey.

CHAPTER 23

THINNING, TOPPING, RAISING

Bible Verse

"In the year that king Uzziah died I saw also the Lord sitting upon a throne, high and lifted up, and his train filled the temple." — Isaiah 6:1

Introduction

This chapter explores the spiritual processes of thinning, topping, and raising as necessary for personal growth and vision, using biblical narratives and personal reflections to illustrate how these processes are integral to a deeper relationship with God.

Word of Wisdom

"God loves you enough to thin you out so the only one you see is Him." Judy Jacobs

Main Theme

"Thinning, Topping, Raising" describes how God strategically removes distractions and places believers in environments conducive to spiritual growth, enhancing their focus on His presence and purposes.

Key Points

• Thinning involves God removing distractions from our lives to help us focus solely on Him, especially during trials.

• Topping places individuals under the guidance of spiritual mentors to foster growth and prepare them for leadership.

• Raising elevates believers to overcome challenges that were meant to destroy them, turning them into testimonies.

• Each process is designed to cultivate a deeper reliance and faith in God.

• The ultimate goal of these processes is to help believers see God more clearly and fulfill their divine destinies.

Key Themes

• **Thinning as a Focus Mechanism:** The thinning process helps believers focus on God during tumultuous times by stripping away what is unnecessary or distracting. This aligns the believer's vision with God's, ensuring that in moments of crisis, they see God's sovereignty and providence.

- **Topping for Mentorship and Growth:** Topping involves placing believers under the mentorship of seasoned spiritual leaders to cultivate wisdom and maturity. This strategic positioning is crucial for personal development and equipping believers with the tools needed for effective ministry and leadership.

- **Raising Through Trials:** Raising is about elevation through adversity, where challenges meant to harm are turned into opportunities for promotion and testimony, similar to Joseph's story. This process ensures that believers not only survive trials but thrive and assume roles of greater influence and responsibility.

- **Integration of Pruning Processes:** These pruning processes—thinning, topping, and raising—are interrelated and contribute to a holistic development plan orchestrated by God. They are tailored to the individual's journey, ensuring they are prepared for the roles and responsibilities God has for them.

- **Outcome of Divine Pruning:** The ultimate outcome of these pruning processes is a life that bears more fruit, demonstrates greater faith, and exerts a more profound influence on others. As believers undergo these transformations, they become more attuned to God's voice and more effective in their divine assignments.

Conclusion

The chapter "Thinning, Topping, Raising" offers insights into the transformative power of God's pruning processes. By understanding and embracing these spiritual disciplines, believers are prepared to encounter God in deeper ways and are equipped to handle the responsibilities of their divine callings with grace and effectiveness.

CHAPTER 24

REDUCTION, NEWNESS, TIMING, TRUSTING

Bible Verse

"Every branch in Me that does not bear fruit, He takes away; and every branch that bears fruit, He prunes it so that it may bear more fruit." —John 15:2 NASB

Introduction

This chapter delves into the spiritual pruning processes of reduction, newness, timing, and trusting. It illustrates how these stages are necessary for growth and fulfillment of God's purposes, drawing parallels with biblical figures who underwent significant transformations.

Word of Wisdom

"If you feel you are being reduced, you are in good company. Even Jesus was reduced." Judy Jacobs

Main Theme

The chapter explores the various aspects of spiritual pruning that God uses to prepare His followers for greater responsibilities and deeper relationships with Him, emphasizing that these are not punishments but preparations for elevation.

Key Points

• Reduction is necessary to remove distractions and humble us, preparing us for God's use.

• Newness emerges from enduring challenges, allowing believers to be shaped into more effective instruments for God's work.

• Timing in God's plan is crucial; understanding divine timing helps us navigate our spiritual journeys with patience.

• Trusting in God's process is essential for enduring pruning without losing faith.

• These processes are not just about enduring but about flourishing in God's kingdom.

Key Themes

• **Reduction as Preparation for Promotion:** Reduction often precedes spiritual elevation, removing excess and focusing a believer's dependence on God. This mirrors Moses' journey from prince to shepherd, which prepared him for leadership.

- **Newness Through Transformation:** God cultivates a new identity in believers, strong and capable of weathering spiritual battles and leading others. This transformation is crucial for those who are called to lead and make significant impacts, as illustrated by Joshua's leadership after Moses.
- **Importance of Divine Timing:** Understanding and accepting God's timing are crucial in spiritual development. Believers are encouraged to trust God's timing, even when progress seems slow, as it ensures readiness for upcoming challenges and blessings.
- **Trusting the Master Pruner:** Trust in God's perfect knowledge and love is essential during pruning. Believers are reassured that God's intentions are for their growth and benefit, aiming to produce more fruit through their lives.
- **Community and Spiritual Mentorship:** The role of community and mentorship in a believer's life is emphasized as critical during times of pruning. Connecting with others of like faith provides support and wisdom, enhancing personal growth and spiritual resilience.

Conclusion

"Reduction, Newness, Timing, Trusting" reflects on the profound and sometimes painful processes of spiritual pruning necessary for growth and greater fruitfulness. Through personal surrender and trust in God's plan, believers can navigate these phases with assurance, knowing that they are being prepared for greater works and deeper fulfillment in their spiritual journeys.

CHAPTER 25

ALL OF US

Bible Verse

"If any two of you agree on earth concerning anything that they ask, it will be done for them by My Father in heaven." — Matthew 18:19 NKJV

Introduction

This chapter explores the communal nature of faith and the essential role of community support in the journey of prayer. It emphasizes the strength found in collective prayer and support within the Body of Christ.

Word of Wisdom

"In the multitude of counselors there is safety." Judy Jacobs

Main Theme

The chapter underscores the importance of gathering support from a diverse community—family, church, and friends—to navigate the challenges of life and faith, reflecting on the collective strength provided through unified prayer and support.

Key Points

• Collective prayer strengthens and amplifies individual efforts.

• Spiritual support spans from family to the wider church community.

• Experienced mentors and leaders are crucial for effective spiritual guidance.

• Unity in prayer reflects the biblical principle of strength in numbers.

• The journey of faith is a communal, not solitary, endeavor.

Key Themes

• **The Power of Agreement in Prayer:** Prayer gains profound strength when shared among believers, as mutual agreement in prayer invokes God's promise of action. This communal aspect of prayer not only bolsters faith but also fosters a deeper sense of belonging and purpose within the church community.

- **Importance of Experienced Guidance:** Just as skilled pruning enhances growth, experienced spiritual mentors play a crucial role in guiding believers through their spiritual journey. Their wisdom helps in making precise adjustments that align individuals more closely with God's will.
- **The Role of Family and Friends:** Support from family and trusted friends is indispensable, acting as a spiritual and emotional backbone that upholds one during trials. This network is vital in maintaining faith and perseverance through challenging times.
- **Navigating Narrow Paths with Support:** The Christian walk often involves navigating narrow and challenging paths that require steadfast faith and endurance. Community support provides the encouragement and confirmation needed to continue forward despite obstacles.
- **Collective Strength in Spiritual Battles:** There is immense power in the collective faith of the community, which can lead to miraculous outcomes in spiritual warfare. This unity is essential for overcoming larger adversities that may seem insurmountable individually.

Conclusion

"All of Us" reaffirms the significance of collective support in the life of a believer. It calls on individuals to cherish and seek out community connections, emphasizing how the shared journey not only enriches the faith experience but is essential for overcoming the challenges and achieving the promises God has laid out for each believer.

CHAPTER 26

DOWN PAYMENT

Bible Verse

"For all of God's promises have been fulfilled in Christ with a resounding 'Yes!' And through Christ, our 'Amen' ascends to God for His glory." — 2 Corinthians 1:20 NLT

Introduction

This chapter explores the concept of the Holy Spirit as God's initial deposit in our lives, guaranteeing His promises and presence. It draws an analogy between a financial down payment and the spiritual assurance we receive through the Holy Spirit.

Word of Wisdom

"The Holy Spirit is our down payment of something that is even greater to come." Judy Jacobs

Main Theme

Highlighting the continuous and steadfast presence of the Holy Spirit, the chapter reassures us of God's constant company and the guaranteed fulfillment of His promises.

Key Points

• The Holy Spirit is a continual reminder of God's presence and promises.

• He equips and enables us to stand firm in our faith.

• Jesus promised the Holy Spirit as a Comforter who would be with and in believers.

• The Holy Spirit's role is multifaceted—comforter, counselor, guide, and more.

• Through the Holy Spirit, believers have a foretaste of heavenly joy and peace.

Key Themes

- **Ever-present Comfort and Guidance:** The Holy Spirit acts as a perpetual counselor and guide, comforting us in trials and leading us in truth. His presence assures us that we are never alone, providing a tangible experience of God's promises every moment.
- **Guarantee of Divine Promises:** Just as a down payment secures a future purchase, the Holy Spirit secures our spiritual

inheritance, ensuring that what God has promised will indeed come to pass. This assurance encourages believers to live with confidence and anticipation of God's faithful fulfillment.

- **Spiritual Empowerment in Daily Life:** The indwelling of the Holy Spirit empowers believers to live out their faith dynamically. He transforms our daily experiences, helping us to manifest the fruit of the Spirit and engage effectively in spiritual warfare.

- **Role of the Holy Spirit in Jesus's Ministry:** Reflecting on Jesus's limitations in human form, the chapter emphasizes how the Holy Spirit now operates without those constraints, enabling Him to be omnipresent in the lives of believers, thus magnifying the reach and impact of Christ's ministry.

- **Personal Assurance and Spiritual Security:** The Holy Spirit's role as a down payment is personal and intimate, providing believers with security and assurance in their spiritual journey. This foundational truth helps believers navigate life with a deep-seated peace and joy.

Conclusion

"Down Payment" reassures us of the steadfast presence and power of the Holy Spirit in our lives as a foretaste of what is to come in eternity. It encourages believers to rely on this divine presence as both a comfort and a guarantee of the greater glory that awaits in God's eternal kingdom.

CHAPTER 27

PROMISES MADE
AND KEPT

Bible Verse

"This day you will be with Me in paradise." – Luke
23:43

Introduction

This chapter explores the enduring power of prayer, illustrating how even when circumstances appear dire, God's promises hold true. It shares a personal testimony to reinforce the belief that God answers prayers, often in unexpected ways.

Word of Wisdom

"It is never too late for God to answer your prayers. As long as there is breath, there is hope." Judy Jacobs

Main Theme

The chapter underscores the concept of God's faithfulness in fulfilling His promises, using a real-life example to demonstrate the transformative power of prayer and God's ability to intervene in critical moments.

Key Points

• Prayer's impact transcends generations, evidenced by a mother's prayers for her children's salvation.

• God's timing in answering prayers can seem mysterious but is always perfect.

• Divine intervention can occur in life's darkest moments, offering salvation and fulfillment of prayers.

• Personal testimonies affirm the power and reach of persistent prayer.

• The Holy Spirit plays a crucial role in guiding and supporting believers through their challenges.

Key Themes

- **Enduring Power of Prayer:** The story of Johnny, who turned to God in his final moments, exemplifies that prayers can resonate and find their fulfillment long after they are offered. This theme reassures believers that their prayers carry weight and potential, even beyond their immediate circumstances.
- **Divine Timing and Intervention:** The narrative highlights that God's

interventions are timed to achieve the greatest impact, as seen in the dramatic rescue and salvation of a soul at the brink of death. This illustrates that God is active and responsive, working behind the scenes to orchestrate outcomes that align with His divine will.

- **Impact of Faithful Intercession:** The faith and perseverance in prayer by family members play a pivotal role in the spiritual outcomes of their loved ones. This theme encourages believers to persist in prayer, trusting that their intercessions will bear fruit in due time.

- **The Transformative Moment of Salvation:** The moment of Johnny's salvation serves as a powerful testament to the idea that no one is beyond the reach of God's grace, reinforcing the concept that the last moments can define a destiny when met with faith and repentance.

- **Legacy of Prayer:** The mother's enduring prayers for her children, which continue to resonate after her passing, teach that the spiritual legacy one leaves through prayer can have eternal implications, influencing generations and outcomes far beyond one's earthly life.

Conclusion

"Promises Made and Kept" imparts a message of hope and relentless faith, reminding readers of the profound impact of continued prayer and God's unwavering commitment to fulfill His promises. It encourages readers to maintain their faith and prayers, emphasizing that God's timing is perfect and His plans are always for our ultimate good.

CHAPTER 28

BETTER IS THE END

Bible Verse

"This day the Lord will deliver you into my hands, and I'll strike you down and cut off your head... All those gathered here will know that it is not by sword or spear that the Lord saves; for the battle is the Lord's, and he will give all of you into our hands." – 1 Samuel 17:46-47 NIV

Introduction

This chapter emphasizes the power of divine prophecy and the certainty of God's promises, encouraging believers to have confidence that what God has shown them about the future will indeed come to pass. It uses the story of David and Goliath as a powerful example of faith in action.

Word of Wisdom

"Prophesy to your children, to your marriage, and believe for the impossible to

happen. Your words are powerful!" Judy Jacobs

Main Theme

Focusing on the concept that God declares the end from the beginning, this chapter explores how true faith involves trusting and declaring God's promises, even when immediate circumstances seem contrary.

Key Points

• God declares the end from the beginning, providing visions of His promises fulfilled.

• Faith involves speaking out God's revelations confidently, believing in their manifestation.

• Sharing visions and dreams should be done with like-minded believers to reinforce spiritual support.

• Prophetic declarations, as exemplified by David before Goliath, can lead to miraculous victories.

• Maintaining faith in God's promises involves continual proclamation and visualization of the victory ahead.

Key Themes

- **Visions as Promises from God:** God often provides clear visions of future blessings as a way to bolster faith. These visions serve as direct communications from God that what He has promised will indeed come to fruition, reinforcing the believer's resolve to trust and wait for God's timing.

- **The Power of Prophetic Declaration:** By vocally declaring God's promises as already fulfilled, believers align themselves with God's will, setting spiritual forces in motion to bring about these declarations. This mirrors the Biblical account of David, who prophesied his victory over Goliath before it physically occurred.
- **Selective Sharing of Divine Insights:** The chapter advises caution in sharing divine revelations, suggesting that such insights should only be shared with those who share similar faith and understanding. This selective sharing is important to nurture and protect the integrity of divine visions.
- **Faith's Role in Overcoming Challenges:** Just as David faced Goliath with unwavering faith and prophetic declaration, believers are encouraged to face their own giants with the same boldness, trusting in the ultimate victory promised by God.
- **Endurance in Faith:** The ultimate message is that enduring faith, characterized by consistent and bold declarations of God's promises, leads to seeing these promises manifest in reality. This endurance is crucial in bridging the gap between divine promise and earthly reality.

Conclusion

"Better Is the End" provides profound insights into the process of prophetic declaration and its necessity in the life of a believer. By maintaining a focus on the promises of God rather than current circumstances, believers are empowered to experience the fulfillment of God's perfect plans for their lives.

CHAPTER 29

CONVERGENCE

Bible Verse

"To everything there is a season, a time for every purpose under heaven." – Ecclesiastes 3:1

Introduction

This chapter explores the concept of convergence, where different elements come together in a divinely orchestrated sequence to fulfill God's purposes. It emphasizes that nothing happens by chance but is part of a larger, God-ordained plan.

Word of Wisdom

"Trust the timing of your life; trust the miraculous convergence of events God orchestrates." Judy Jacobs

Main Theme

The main theme revolves around the intricate way God aligns circumstances, relationships, and events in life, reflecting His perfect timing and plans for each individual.

Key Points

• Convergence describes events and relationships coming together in divine order.

• The complex genealogy required for each person's birth is a type of convergence.

• Personal experiences often highlight God's hand in guiding life's direction.

• Psalm 139 emphasizes God's intimate involvement and pre-knowledge of our lives.

• Trusting God's timing is crucial as He orchestrates our life's convergences.

Key Themes

- **Divine Orchestration of Life Events:** Every individual's existence is the result of thousands of convergences over generations—events that were ordained by God to bring about each unique life. This realization brings a profound understanding of the significance and purpose behind our daily experiences and encounters.
- **Impact of Personal Loss and Prayer:** Personal stories, such as the author's

reflection on the death of a family member, illustrate how pivotal moments can lead to deeper spiritual insights and life changes. These events often catalyze a more focused pursuit of God's plans through prayer, showing how personal loss can contribute to spiritual convergence.

- **Scriptural Foundations for Convergence:** Scriptures like Psalm 139 and Ecclesiastes 3:1 provide a biblical foundation that reassures believers of God's sovereign control over the timing and details of their lives. These verses affirm that God's knowledge and plans encompass all aspects of our existence.

- **Strategic Spiritual Practices for Facilitating Convergence:** The author highlights practical steps such as fasting and specific prayer strategies aimed at inviting divine intervention and guidance, suggesting that active spiritual engagement can influence the convergence of God's promises in one's life.

- **Recognizing and Responding to Divine Timing:** Understanding and accepting God's timing is essential for recognizing convergence when it occurs. The author encourages readers to remain patient and faithful, trusting that God's arrangements, though sometimes inscrutable, are always aimed at fulfilling His perfect plan for each life.

Conclusion

"Convergence" emphasizes the beautiful complexity of God's plans and the assurance that every aspect of our lives is part of a divine tapestry. By understanding and trusting in God's timing and plans, we can better appreciate the moments of convergence that shape our destiny. The chapter calls on believers to maintain faith in God's overarching purpose, knowing that every convergence leads us closer to fulfilling our God-given potential and purpose.

CHAPTER 30

HIS PLAN

Bible Verse

"Wait on the Lord: be of good courage, and he shall strengthen thine heart: wait, I say, on the Lord." – Psalm 27:14

Introduction

This chapter explores the concept of divine convergence in life's journey, emphasizing the importance of waiting for God's perfect timing and following His plans rather than our own.

Word of Wisdom

"Hell will have to freeze over now before I go back home and go back on what God has spoken over my life." This statement reflects a deep commitment to pur-

suing God's call despite challenges. Judy Jacobs

Main Theme

The theme centers on the significance of God-ordained convergence, where life events are intricately woven together by divine guidance, leading to fulfilling God's purposes for individuals.

Key Points

• God orchestrates divine convergences in our lives, often described as "God moments."

• Challenges and opposition are tools used to test faith and commitment to God's plan.

• Significant life changes, like the call to ministry, require spiritual readiness and openness.

• Negative advice or discouragement from others can be a catalyst for reaffirming one's divine calling.

• Waiting on God's timing proves crucial in experiencing His planned convergence.

• Personal stories of convergence affirm the faithfulness of God in orchestrating life events.

Key Themes

- **Divine Timing and Life's Direction:** Understanding and accepting God's timing is crucial in recognizing the convergence of life events. The author's personal journey illustrates how God's timing perfectly aligns with career opportunities and spiritual growth, encouraging readers to trust in divine sequences even when immediate circumstances seem discouraging.

- **The Role of Spiritual Antennas in Recognizing God's Plan:** Staying spiritually attuned is essential for recognizing and seizing the God moments that define our destiny. The author stresses the importance of being spiritually vigilant to discern and participate in God's plans, avoiding distractions and discouragements that can derail divine purposes.
- **Impact of Opposition and Challenges on Spiritual Growth:** Facing opposition and challenges is often a part of God's plan to strengthen faith and foster perseverance. The author's experiences highlight how criticism and negative feedback were used to deepen her resolve and commitment to God's call, serving as a reminder that challenges often precede significant breakthroughs.
- **Waiting on God's Promises:** The narrative reinforces the virtue of patience in waiting on God's promises, using scriptural references and personal anecdotes to illustrate how premature actions can lead to chaos, while waiting on God ensures alignment with His perfect will.
- **The Power of Prophetic Declarations in Achieving God's Plan:** Prophetic

declarations are portrayed as vital tools for bringing about God's convergence. The author encourages readers to speak life and faith into their circumstances, believing in the power of spoken words to manifest God's promises and change reality.

Conclusion

"His Plan" reminds us that God's timing and design for our lives are perfect. Through a series of personal anecdotes and biblical insights, the chapter encourages readers to trust in God's plan, emphasizing that every aspect of our lives, including the challenges, is part of a divine convergence leading to our ultimate purpose. It calls on believers to remain faithful and patient, trusting that God's plans are unfolding perfectly in His timing.

CHAPTER 31

IN-BETWEEN MOMENTS

Bible Verse

"I will give him the key to the house of David—the highest position in the royal court. When he opens doors, no one will be able to close them; when he closes doors, no one will be able to open them." – Isaiah 22:22 NLT

Introduction

This chapter delves into the significance of the transitional periods in our lives, often experienced as waiting periods between God's opened and closed doors, emphasizing the spiritual growth and preparation they entail.

Word of Wisdom

"You will be the most tempted to quit when you are the closest to your calling, to your open doors, and to answered

prayer." – This highlights the critical nature of perseverance in the face of stagnation. Judy Jacobs

Main Theme

The theme focuses on understanding and appreciating the "in-between" moments—those periods of waiting and uncertainty between life's significant changes and God's promises being fulfilled.

Key Points

• The in-between moments are critical transitions between significant life changes.

• These periods often feel like stagnation but are rich in spiritual growth.

• Patience and endurance are vital in navigating these times.

• God's timing is crucial; rushing can lead to chaos.

• Transitioning from one phase to another requires divine alignment and readiness.

• These periods prepare us for the next phase of our lives as part of God's perfect plan.

Key Themes

• **The Role of Patience and Trust in God's Timing:** During the in-between times, the necessity of patience is paramount. These periods serve as a preparation for what is next, and rushing through them or abandoning the process prematurely can disrupt God's perfect timing and plan for our lives.

- **Spiritual Growth During Transition:** These transitional phases, though challenging, are fertile grounds for spiritual growth and deepening faith. They are opportunities to develop a closer relationship with God, understanding that He is working behind the scenes even when no progress is apparent.
- **The Importance of Divine Preparation:** In-between moments are not just times of waiting but of active divine preparation. They are designed to equip us spiritually, emotionally, and sometimes physically for what lies ahead, ensuring we are ready to step through the next open door fully prepared.
- **Dealing with Uncertainty and Stagnation:** Feeling stuck is a common experience in these periods. The chapter discusses strategies for dealing with the feelings of stagnation, emphasizing the importance of remaining faithful and continuing to work towards personal and spiritual development.
- **Recognizing and Responding to God's Timing:** The recognition that God's timing often does not align with our expectations is crucial. The chapter encourages readers to align their desires with God's will, trusting that He knows

the best times for each season to begin and end.

Conclusion

"In-Between Moments" teaches that the periods of waiting between life's significant events are not to be overlooked or undervalued. They are divinely orchestrated times where patience, growth, and preparation occur, ensuring that when the next door opens, we are ready to walk through it aligned with God's will. These moments, though often challenging, are filled with potential for deep spiritual insights and are essential for moving into God's promises with maturity and readiness.

CHAPTER 32

SEASON OF CHALLENGE

Bible Verse

"I will give him the key to the house of David—the highest position in the royal court. When he opens doors, no one will be able to close them; when he closes doors, no one will be able to open them." – Isaiah 22:22 NLT

Introduction

This chapter explores the concept of navigating through challenging seasons in life by recognizing them as necessary periods of growth and preparation for future blessings.

Word of Wisdom

"Sometimes you have to sow a seed into your season of adversity to announce

to God and all of hell how thankful you are for the past season." Judy Jacobs

Main Theme

The theme discusses the power of positive action and faith during difficult times, highlighting how challenges can be transformative and lead to greater opportunities.

Key Points

• Challenging seasons are often platforms for growth and pivotal changes.

• Sowing into adversity can lead to breakthroughs and defeat the enemy's plans.

• God's timing is crucial in the transition from one season to the next.

• Maintaining faith and integrity is essential during tough times.

• Every challenge faced is a stepping stone towards fulfilling God's promises.

Key Themes

• **Transformative Power of Adversity:** Seasons of challenge are not just obstacles but opportunities for spiritual growth and character development. By facing these challenges with faith and integrity, individuals can transform adverse situations into testimonies of God's faithfulness.

- **Strategic Responses to Challenges:** Acting strategically during difficult times, such as sowing seeds of faith and giving back, can catalyze positive changes. These actions are based on biblical principles that emphasize the importance of faithfulness and stewardship, even in adversity.
- **God's Timing in Life Transitions:** Understanding and accepting God's timing are crucial during transitional periods. These moments require patience and trust, recognizing that God orchestrates the timing of every season for a greater purpose.
- **Importance of Maintaining Integrity:** In the midst of challenges, maintaining integrity and steadfast faith can safeguard one's spiritual journey and ensure alignment with God's plans. This integrity acts as a testimony to others and strengthens personal character.
- **Encouragement and Hope in Adversity:** The chapter provides encouragement to persevere through difficult seasons, highlighting that these are not permanent and serve a divine purpose. It reassures readers that with faith, the challenges will lead to eventual victory and fulfillment of God's promises.

Conclusion

"Season of Challenge" reinforces the idea that challenges are not merely hardships but divine appointments that shape an individual's destiny. By embracing these seasons with faith and understanding their purpose, one can navigate through them with grace and emerge stronger, ready to enter a new season equipped and renewed. The chapter calls readers to trust in God's plan, emphasizing that every season has a divine purpose that aligns with greater blessings and fulfillment.

CHAPTER 33

FOR REAL

Bible Verse

"Praise be to the God and Father of our Lord Jesus Christ! In his great mercy he has given us new birth into a living hope through the resurrection of Jesus Christ from the dead." – 1 Peter 1:3 NIV

Introduction

This chapter explores the concept of maintaining hope in the face of life's inevitable challenges, encouraging a perspective shift towards positivity and resilience.

Word of Wisdom

"Life happens. But there is good news —God is also real and there is hope in the midst of all of life." Judy Jacobs

Main Theme

The main theme revolves around the understanding and acceptance of life's challenges, emphasizing the power of maintaining hope and a positive outlook through faith in God.

Key Points

• Life is full of inevitable challenges like aging, family conflicts, financial troubles, sickness, and loss.

• These challenges test our faith and resilience, pushing us to maintain hope.

• Hope in God provides a living, active presence that supports us through difficulties.

• True hope is characterized by a confidence in God's promises, anchoring us in trials.

• We must adopt a mature, yet hopeful attitude to navigate life's realities effectively.

Key Themes

- **Reality of Life's Challenges:** Life's challenges are diverse and inevitable, ranging from personal aging and financial difficulties to global crises like pandemics. These challenges can induce stress and despair, but they are also opportunities for growth and deepening faith.
- **Maintaining Hope Amidst Trials:** The ability to maintain hope during difficult

times is crucial. Hope is not just wishful thinking but a robust, faith-based confidence in God's promises. It acts as a buffer against despair, providing the strength to endure and overcome adversities.

- **Impact of Attitude on Perception:** Our attitude significantly affects how we perceive and react to life's challenges. A positive, hope-filled attitude can transform our experience of difficult times, turning obstacles into opportunities for growth and testimonial development.
- **Spiritual Growth through Adversity:** Adversity is a potent teacher that presents the tests of life first, followed by the lessons. By embracing these lessons with hope and faith, we can achieve profound spiritual growth and a closer relationship with God.
- **Hope as a Testament of Faith:** Hope stands as a testament to our faith in God's plan. It is the belief in the unseen, the trust in God's timing, and the expectation of His intervention that sustains us through the "in-between" times and leads to spiritual renewal and miracles.

Conclusion

The chapter "For Real" serves as a poignant reminder of the transformative power of hope in navigating the realities of life. By choosing to see the glass as half full and embracing each challenge with a spirit of hope, we align ourselves with God's promises, fostering resilience and joy amidst life's inevitable trials.

CHAPTER 34

IT IS WELL

Bible Verse

"Is it well with you?" – 2 Kings 4:26 NKJV

Introduction

This chapter explores the story of the Shunammite woman from 2 Kings 4, using her response to profound personal crisis as a powerful example of faith and persistence in the face of adversity.

Word of Wisdom

"Did I desire a son of my lord? Did I not say, Do not deceive me?"

Main Theme

The chapter examines the depth of unwavering faith and the concept of claiming God's promises even when faced with despair and apparent defeat.

Key Points

• The Shunammite woman was promised a son by Elisha, which miraculously came to pass.

• Tragedy struck when her young son suddenly died, testing her faith profoundly.

• Despite her grief, she sought Elisha, declaring "It is well" as a statement of faith.

• She insisted on Elisha's presence rather than accepting the proxy service of his servant.

• Her persistence and faith were rewarded when Elisha revived her son, reaffirming God's promise.

Key Themes

- **Unwavering Faith Amid Tragedy:** The Shunammite woman's journey from receiving a divine promise to facing her son's death showcases the raw reality of clinging to faith amid personal crisis. Her actions reflect a deep belief in God's power to restore life, illustrating her spiritual resolve and resilience.

- **Interactions with Divine Promise:** The chapter delves into the dynamics between receiving prophetic promises and experiencing their fulfillment. It highlights the emotional and spiritual rollercoaster that believers may undergo while waiting on God's timing, emphasizing the importance of maintaining faith even when circumstances seem dire.

- **Challenge of Maintaining Belief:** The narrative underscores the challenge of maintaining belief in God's promises through the testing of one's faith by life's harsh realities. It illustrates how true faith often requires a tenacity to hold onto God's word despite overwhelming despair.
- **The Role of Spiritual Leaders:** The interaction between the Shunammite woman and Elisha emphasizes the role of spiritual leaders in nurturing and sometimes directly intervening in the faith journeys of their followers. It portrays how leaders are sometimes called to reaffirm God's promises personally and powerfully.
- **Miraculous Outcomes Through Persistence:** This theme explores the outcome of the woman's unwavering insistence for a miracle, serving as a testament to the power of persistence in faith. It suggests that miraculous outcomes often follow the refusal to accept defeat, encouraging believers to actively pursue God's intervention.

Conclusion

"It Is Well" serves as an inspiring testament to the power of faith in overcoming life's most harrowing

challenges. The Shunammite woman's story
encourages readers to hold steadfastly to God's
promises, pursuing faith with boldness and
assurance, and proclaiming "It is well" in the midst
of storms, trusting in God's ultimate plan for
restoration and blessing.

CHAPTER 35

ALL WAS WELL

Bible Verse

"So he arose and followed her." – 2 Kings
4:30 NKJV

Introduction

This chapter focuses on the power of persistent faith, illustrated through the story of the Shunammite woman and her son in 2 Kings 4. It emphasizes the importance of relentless prayer and trusting in divine timing, even in the face of despair.

Word of Wisdom

"You're still on the right track." Judy Jacobs

Main Theme

The narrative underscores the concept that life's greatest trials can lead to profound spiritual victories when met with unwavering faith and the expectation of God's intervention.

Key Points

• The Shunammite woman's son, initially dead, was revived by Elisha after her persistent faith and action.

• She expressed unshakeable faith by insisting on Elisha's personal intervention, despite initial proposals for indirect help.

• The woman's declaration of "It is well" symbolizes profound faith in God's promise, regardless of circumstances.

• Her journey from receiving a divine promise to confronting the child's death and ultimately witnessing his resurrection teaches about the perseverance needed in faith.

• The narrative closes with the boy's miraculous recovery, affirming the power of faith and prophetic assurance.

Key Themes

• **Relentless Pursuit of Divine Promises:** The chapter portrays the Shunammite woman's relentless pursuit of the prophet Elisha to restore her son as a testament to her faith in God's promises. This act emphasizes that spiritual victories often require action in faith beyond passive belief.

- **Challenges as Catalysts for Spiritual Growth:** Her challenges transformed into a testament of faith, illustrating how believers can leverage divine promises against seemingly insurmountable odds. The story encourages readers to view obstacles as opportunities for showcasing God's miraculous power.

- **The Role of Prophetic Assurance in Sustaining Faith:** Through Elisha's prophecy and subsequent actions, the chapter explores how prophetic words can anchor our faith during crises. It emphasizes the importance of holding onto these assurances as tangible links to God's plans for our lives.

- **Impact of Divine Intervention:** The revival of the Shunammite's son highlights the transformative impact of divine intervention, showing that faith not only changes circumstances but also strengthens our spiritual resolve and commitment to God's word.

- **Faith's Victory Over Despair:** By focusing on the moment the child revives, sneezing seven times and opening his eyes, the chapter symbolizes the sudden and profound victories faith can achieve over death, despair, and defeat, inspiring believers to maintain hope against hope.

Conclusion

"All Was Well" serves as a profound reminder of the effectiveness of steadfast faith and the reality of miracles in our spiritual journey. It encourages readers to embrace a posture of unwavering belief and persistent pursuit of God's promises, assuring them that with God, all things can indeed be well, regardless of current appearances.

CHAPTER 36

HIS PEACE, HIS PRESENCE

Bible Verse

"You will keep in perfect peace those whose minds are steadfast, because they trust in you." – Isaiah 26:3 AMPC

Introduction

This chapter explores the profound peace available through maintaining a focus on God's presence despite the chaos of life. It emphasizes the importance of internal serenity over external calm, proposing that peace is found not in the absence of trouble but in the continual awareness of God's proximity.

Word of Wisdom

"Anything that costs you your peace is too expensive." Judy Jacobs

Main Theme

The chapter underscores the necessity of keeping one's mind and heart centered on God as a strategy for accessing divine peace, highlighting that true tranquility is a result of spiritual focus rather than circumstantial stability.

Key Points

• True peace is defined not by the absence of conflict but by the presence of God amidst life's challenges.

• Keeping one's focus on God ensures peace because it aligns one's spirit with divine reassurance and calm.

• External conflicts and challenges test our peace but focusing on God's presence provides the strength to overcome.

• Spiritual practices like prayer and meditation on scripture are crucial for maintaining peace.

• Peace is a gift from God, distinct from worldly peace, offering deep and lasting serenity.

Key Themes

• **The Nature of True Peace:** True peace is achieved through a constant mental and spiritual focus on God, rather than attempting to control or avoid life's inevitable challenges. This peace is profoundly rooted in the assurance of God's omnipresence and omnipotence, providing stability regardless of external circumstances.

- **Strategies for Maintaining Peace:** Intentionally centering one's heart and mind on God's presence involves regular spiritual disciplines like prayer, meditation on the Scriptures, and cultivating a personal relationship with God. These practices empower individuals to withstand and rise above the turmoil and distractions of life.

- **The Cost of Losing Peace:** The chapter discusses the high cost of situations or relationships that disturb our peace, advocating for a life that prioritizes spiritual tranquility over all else. It stresses the importance of discerning and sometimes distancing oneself from peace-stealers.

- **The Power of a Peaceful Mindset:** A peaceful mindset enables believers to handle life's stresses with grace and confidence. It acts as a buffer against despair and negativity, fostering an environment where spiritual growth and personal development can flourish.

- **The Impact of Divine Peace on Daily Living:** Living in God's peace influences one's interactions and decisions, promoting harmony and reducing strife. It also enhances one's ability to be a positive influence on others, extending the peace one experiences from God into broader community and relational dynamics.

Conclusion

"His Peace, His Presence" serves as a vital reminder of the transformative power of maintaining focus on God amidst life's tumult. It calls on readers to cultivate and cherish the peace that comes from divine presence, assuring them of God's ability to sustain and protect them through all of life's seasons.

CHAPTER 37

THINK ABOUT...

Bible Verse

"Finally, brothers and sisters, whatever is true, whatever is noble, whatever is right, whatever is pure, whatever is lovely, whatever is admirable—if anything is excellent or praiseworthy—think about such things." – Philippians 4:8 NLT

Introduction

This chapter emphasizes the power of focusing thoughts on positive and godly things amid the overwhelming noise of daily life. It discusses the importance of guarding one's mind against negative influences and filling it with the truth of God's Word.

Word of Wisdom

"Anything that costs you your peace is too expensive." – This advice underscores the value of maintaining peace

through careful control over one's
thoughts and inputs.

Main Theme

The central theme is the transformative power of meditating on what is pure, lovely, and admirable, which aligns one's thoughts with God's character, influencing mood, behavior, and ultimately, life's outcomes.

Key Points

• Daily life is inundated with various forms of information that can affect mental and spiritual health.

• The Bible provides a blueprint for filtering thoughts to ensure they are wholesome and edifying.

• Singing and praising God can positively influence one's thoughts and emotional state.

• Focusing on spiritual truths can fortify the mind against negative influences.

• The Apostle Paul provides guidance on maintaining peace through thoughtful meditation on godly virtues.

Key Themes

• **Impact of Media and Thoughts on Spiritual Well-being:** Consuming negative media can lead to disturbed peace, whereas engaging with uplifting content and focusing on spiritual truths can enhance one's mental and spiritual health. This practice is crucial in maintaining a positive outlook and spiritual growth.

- **Biblical Strategy for Thought Management:** Scripture advises believers to actively manage their thoughts by focusing on the positive attributes of God and His creation. This practice not only aligns one with divine truth but also builds a foundation of inner peace and resilience against life's challenges.

- **The Role of Worship in Thought Life:** Engaging in worship and spiritual songs is not only an act of devotion but also a strategic approach to cultivating a positive mindset. This form of expression has a profound impact on emotional well-being and can transform one's outlook on life.

- **Practical Application of Scriptural Principles:** Implementing the advice of Philippians 4:8 involves a deliberate effort to focus on the positive, which requires daily commitment to studying the Word and prayer. This commitment helps sustain a spiritual defense against negativity and despair.

- **Outcome of Maintaining a Godly Focus:** Maintaining a focus on godly themes leads to a life characterized by peace and positivity, impacting personal well-being and influencing those around us. It is an active stance against the negativity pervasive in society and asserts the power of faith in everyday life.

Conclusion

"Think About..." serves as a compelling reminder of the importance of guarding one's thoughts and focusing on the goodness of God. It encourages readers to take active steps in shaping their mental landscapes by choosing to dwell on what is pure, just, and praiseworthy, leading to a life of peace and fulfillment in God's presence.

CHAPTER 38

UNDERCURRENTS

Bible Verse

"Be sober, be vigilant; because your adversary, the devil, as a roaring lion, walketh about, seeking whom he may devour." – 1 Peter 5:8

Introduction

This chapter draws an analogy between the unseen dangers of undercurrents on a serene beach and the spiritual threats that believers face. It emphasizes the need for vigilance and spiritual awareness to navigate these hidden dangers effectively.

Word of Wisdom

"Never let your guard down for the enemy to see where you are most vulnerable." Judy Jacobs

143

Main Theme

The main theme explores the spiritual undercurrents that threaten to undermine believers, emphasizing the need for constant vigilance, prayer, and reliance on God's Word to overcome these challenges.

Key Points

• The peaceful appearance of life can be deceptive, masking underlying dangers.

• Spiritual vigilance is crucial; the devil is constantly seeking to devour the unwary.

• After achieving spiritual victories, believers must guard against complacency.

• Jesus' temptation in the wilderness illustrates the relentless nature of satanic attacks.

• Spiritual warfare requires constant readiness and recourse to Scripture.

• Victory in Christ is assured through faith and steadfastness in facing spiritual challenges.

Key Themes

• **Continuous Spiritual Warfare:** The chapter illustrates that like natural undercurrents, spiritual threats are not always visible but can be deadly. Believers must stay alert to spiritual dangers and resist complacency, especially after victories, as the enemy often attacks when least expected.

- **The Role of Scripture in Combatting Spiritual Attacks:**
- Scripture is the believer's primary weapon against spiritual deceptions and attacks. The narrative of Jesus countering Satan's temptations with Scripture underscores its power and the need to internalize it to maintain spiritual integrity and victory.
- **The Importance of Spiritual Vigilance:** Staying spiritually vigilant involves recognizing that the enemy uses subtle and indirect methods. Believers must be sober and watchful, understanding that spiritual undercurrents can shift swiftly and require a dynamic and persistent faith response.
- **Overcoming Through Christ:** The assurance of overcoming spiritual undercurrents is rooted in the power of Jesus Christ, who has already overcome the world. This truth provides believers with hope and the strength to continue fighting against spiritual adversities.
- **Maintaining Peace Through Spiritual Authority:** Even amidst spiritual warfare, believers can maintain peace by focusing on Christ and His promises. Understanding and exercising spiritual authority through prayer and the Word helps manage the threats posed by spiritual undercurrents effectively.

Conclusion

"Undercurrents" calls believers to a deeper awareness of the spiritual battles they face daily. By drawing lessons from biblical examples and the teachings of Christ, it encourages a proactive stance in spiritual warfare, emphasizing faith, scripture, and vigilance as keys to sustaining victory and peace in the Christian journey.

CHAPTER 39

THE SOUL'S EYE

Bible Verse

"For as he thinketh in his heart, so is he" –
Proverbs 23:7.

Introduction

This chapter explores the profound impact of our thoughts and words on our spiritual and everyday lives. It emphasizes the power of the conscience and the Holy Spirit in guiding our actions and shaping our reality.

Word of Wisdom

"Your conscience will always direct you to God's perfect Word and instruct you in what you really should do." Judy Jacobs

Main Theme

The main theme focuses on the importance of aligning thoughts with God's Word to navigate life's challenges effectively, highlighting the role of the conscience as a guide and protector.

Key Points

• The conscience acts as the soul's eye, directing our focus toward God's standards.

• Continuous renewal of the mind through Scripture is essential for spiritual alignment.

• The words we speak can have a lasting impact on our lives and those of future generations.

• God offers wisdom generously to those who seek it, aiding in discernment and decision-making.

• True peace and security come from focusing on God, regardless of external circumstances.

Key Themes

- **Conscience as a Spiritual Guide** The conscience, influenced by the Holy Spirit, helps discern right from wrong, guiding decisions and actions according to God's will. It serves not only as a moral compass but also as a source of conviction when one strays from God's path.
- **Power and Impact of Words:** Words have the power to shape reality, influence generations, and determine spiritual health. The chapter underscores the

necessity of guarding one's speech, using Jesus' example of countering Satan's temptations with Scripture.

- **Renewing the Mind:** Spiritual renewal through engaging with the Bible and maintaining a prayerful attitude is crucial for overcoming negative thoughts and temptations. This renewal process empowers believers to live out God's perfect will.
- **Wisdom from Above:** Seeking and receiving divine wisdom is pivotal for understanding and fulfilling God's purposes. This wisdom, which is pure and peace-loving, is essential for making decisions that align with God's will.
- **Navigating Life's Challenges with God's Perspective:** By focusing thoughts on what is true and godly, believers can overcome negative influences and maintain a positive spiritual trajectory. The chapter encourages readers to cultivate a mindset that constantly seeks God's guidance and wisdom.

Conclusion

"The Soul's Eye" calls believers to a deeper commitment to guard their minds and hearts by focusing on God's Word and relying on the Holy Spirit. By doing so, they can transform their thoughts, words, and actions to reflect God's will, ultimately leading a life marked by divine wisdom and peace.

CHAPTER 40

EXCEEDINGLY
ABUNDANTLY

Bible Verse

"Now to Him who is able to do exceedingly abundantly above all that we ask or think" – Ephesians 3:20 NKJV.

Introduction

This chapter emphasizes the boundless capabilities of God to surpass our expectations and prayers, encouraging believers to maintain faith even when faced with life's unpredictable challenges.

Word of Wisdom

"Your confidence is not in your prayers, but in the God who answers prayers." Judy Jacobs

Main Theme

The main theme centers on the power of maintaining a steadfast faith and the expectation of God's intervention, highlighting how He operates beyond our imagination and desires.

Key Points

• Life is unpredictable, but God's faithfulness remains constant.

• Staying rooted in God's Word provides stability amidst chaos.

• Prayer should be accompanied by thanksgiving and expectation.

• God's ability to answer prayers exceeds our own understanding and requests.

• Maintaining peace and handing over anxieties to God is crucial.

• Expectation is key to receiving answers to prayers.

Key Themes

- **Steadfastness in Faith:** In times of turbulence, anchoring oneself in the unshakable truth of God's Word is essential. This foundation enables believers to withstand any life's storms with assurance and peace.
- **Expectancy in Prayer:** Approaching prayer with expectation forms the basis of a dynamic faith life, where trust is placed

not just in the act of praying, but in God's supreme power to answer those prayers in ways that transcend human understanding.

- **The Power of Thanksgiving:** Gratitude in prayer shifts focus from one's challenges to God's capabilities, fostering an atmosphere where faith can grow and God's interventions are welcomed and recognized.
- **Anxiety versus Peace:** The directive to be anxious for nothing encapsulates God's provision for peace. By presenting every concern through prayer and supplication with thanksgiving, believers can experience the peace that surpasses all understanding.
- **God's Infinite Capabilities:** The acknowledgment of God's limitless ability to work beyond our requests encourages believers to dream big and pray boldly, expecting that God can and will do much more than what is asked or imagined.

Conclusion

"Exceedingly Abundantly" uplifts and reassures believers of the limitless nature of God's power and His willingness to intervene miraculously in their lives. It calls for a life of robust faith, anchored in the truth of God's Word, energized by prayerful expectation, and peaceful surrender to His divine will.

www.ingramcontent.com/pod-product-compliance
Lightning Source LLC
Chambersburg PA
CBHW070901160726
48004CB00003B/1196